When Your Plans Fall Through...

God Changes Our Plans to Accomplish His Will

Judy Hampton

When Your Plans Fall Through...
God Changes Our Plans to Accomplish His Will

Published by Wheatmark®
610 East Delano Street, Suite 104
Tucson, Arizona 85705 U.S.A.
www.wheatmark.com

ISBN: 978-1-60494-506-5
LCCN: 2010934098

Contents

To Joani, Ed, Eddy, and Lauren

Thanks for always putting your arms around us
when our plans fall through

The Learning Curve of Change

Let's get right down to it. Who doesn't need to change? Yet when uninvited change invades our life, and especially when the changes are painful, the first response is usually, "Why?" It has taken a good deal of time for me to realize that when my plans fall through, God is about to *come* through!

God changes our plans to accomplish his will. "People can make all kinds of plans, but only the Lord's plans will happen" (Prov. 19:21, NCV). God wants the same thing from us that he wants from the whole universe. He wants to display his presence (and therefore glory) through the way we handle life. After he's changed us, he uses us to minister to someone else going through the same thing. That is how ministry begins.

The glory of God has been present since the beginning of time. In the Old Testament the manifestation of God's glory was displayed through the pillar of cloud and fire that led the Israelites out of captivity. Then the glory cloud stood behind them at night to protect them. His Shekinah glory filled the tabernacle with his presence and appeared continuously for forty years.

Today, God doesn't need a glory cloud. The Triune God; the Father, Son, and Holy Spirit; came packaged in the body of Jesus Christ. In essence, God is saying this about Jesus, "Here is my Glory, here is my outshining, and here is my manifested presence." After Jesus ascended to heaven, the Holy Spirit came upon the believer. Today, God is saying, "If you want to see what I look like, look at

Mary, Barbara, or insert your name here. See how they triumph through trials? They shout my glory."

When we stand before the world, our life should reflect what Jesus said to Philip in John 14, "If you have seen me, you have seen the Father." Or as Paul writes, "But we all, with unveiled face beholding as in a mirror the glory of the Lord, are transformed into the same image from glory to glory, even as from the Lord the Spirit" (2 Cor. 3:18 ASV).

God's glory is displayed most effectively by the way we handle adversity. "Don't be surprised at the fiery trials you are going through, as if something strange were happening to you. Instead be very glad, because these trials will make you partners with Christ in his suffering, and afterward you will have the wonderful joy of sharing his glory when it has been displayed to the whole world" (1 Peter 4:12-13. NASB).

Jesus has something very special in mind for your life. Whatever you're going through has *something* to do with God's glory and a changed life.

Notes:
1. Glory of God, teaching CD 2007, Jennifer Kennedy Dean, Prayinglife.org

ONE

The Beginning of Change

"Everything—connected with that old way of life has to go. It's rotten through and through. Get rid of it! And then take on an entirely new way of life—a God-fashioned life, a life renewed from the inside and working itself into your conduct as God accurately reproduces his character in you."
Ephesians 4:22–24 (MSG)

"You have a spot on your lung," my doctor said rather matter-of-factly after glancing at my chest X-ray.

"What?" My stomach did a flip-flop.

"It's probably nothing, but we'll need to order a CT scan for you just to make sure."

"Do you think I should order a casket from Costco as well? I hear it takes a few weeks to get it."

He smiled and reassured me it was probably nothing, but it did need to be checked out. (I confess I am terribly negligent when it comes to checking with doctors and

1

dealing with health issues. I get a yearly physical about every five years whether I need it or not. The whole thing sort of bores me.)

A week later I had a CT scan and was told the spot was dangerously close to my pulmonary artery, and so I needed to see a specialist.

I called one of my best friends, Cheryl, for some moral support, and she reminded me that her son-in-law, Rob, is a pulmonary specialist at Sharps Hospital in San Diego.

"I'll give him a call and call you right back."

In the meantime, I called my family, close friends and ministry partners and asked for prayer.

Rob agreed to see me immediately. He told me to bring the scan. Two days later we were driving to his office for his opinion and evaluation.

"I can't tell exactly what this is because the scan is very low definition. I'll tell you what I'm going to do. I'll run this by some of my colleagues and get their take on this. We may have to do a biopsy to see if it is cancer."

"How do you do a biopsy on a lung?" I asked, not wanting to know.

"We go through the chest with a needle."

I'd rather jump out of your office window, I thought.

"If this is cancer, I'll have to remove the middle lobe of your lung. You will be out of commission for at least six months."

Wow, that changes everything, I thought. *This isn't something I planned and penciled in my Day-Timer.* The timing stunk. My schedule was jam-packed with obligations. Now everything hung in the balance.

It happened just that quickly to me, and the same thing can happen to you. Let me ask you, has God changed your plans recently? How have you handled this interruption to your otherwise well-planned-out life?

The Beginning of Change

Interruptions are really what change is all about. The cycle of change begins when something external intrudes into our life: an unexpected diagnosis from the doctor, a spouse who wants a divorce, an unplanned pregnancy, a teen who rebels, a financial reversal, a job loss, betrayal, a natural disaster, the death of a loved one, or simply the death of a dream. When these kinds of crises arise, we are prone to question God or blame someone. It's a pattern of behavior even the disciples fell into because they questioned Jesus a lot.

For example, John 9 illustrates this response. One day as Jesus was walking, and he saw a man who had been blind from birth. The disciples asked him, "Rabbi, who sinned, this man or his parents, that he was born blind?"

Jesus answered, "Neither this man nor his parents sinned, but this happened so that the work of God might be displayed in his life."

(In other words, this man was born blind so that they could see how God goes about his business.)

In the same way, consider the changes in your life as being a part of God's plan to display his glory through you. The reality is this is how God works as indicated in Proverbs 19:21, "You can make many plans, but the Lord's purpose will prevail." When we are on the other side of these life changes, we can look back and clearly see his hand.

Painful Change

Now that doesn't mean that change doesn't come without hardship and pain. It can take years to see the hand of God at work in our life circumstances.

Joni Erickson Tada can look back and see God's hand in ways she never expected. But she couldn't see it the day she dove into the Chesapeake Bay for an innocent swim on a hot summer day.

Unaware of how shallow the water was, her head slammed into the sand and immediately she was unable to move her body. After her sister rescued her from drowning, an ambulance took her to the hospital. The diagnosis was grim: a broken neck. This once-vibrant athlete was now a quadriplegic, a prisoner in her own body.

Her initial response was what we would expect. She asked, "Why?" In the months that followed her accident, depression, hopelessness, and anger defined her life. In fact she was mad at everyone, including God. She didn't understand that he was pursuing her.

Over time she came to a place where she surrendered her life to him. He met her right where she was. Her fresh faith drew her into his word, began maturing her, and changed her viewpoint of life. God was transforming her into a woman willing to become his vessel through which he would display his glory.

She went on to start a ministry called Joni and Friends, an organization that accelerates Christian ministry in the disabled community. Her tragedy has been used as a tool to open the Church's eyes to the need for ministries that zero in on the disabled. Today, she speaks internationally. Her disability has been an opportunity to speak of God's saving grace, hope, and sufficiency no matter what a person's limitations are.

Without Joni's accident, these things would have never happened. It was a very important day.

If you look back on your life—as Joni has, do you remember an important day when God changed your life? Or is he currently pursuing you?

Looking Back at Life

When I look back at my life, I see that God was pursing me even as a child. I grew up in a small town and was part of a fairly typical American family. We weren't what you would call a religious family. The only time I heard Jesus' name was when Dad's car wouldn't start, but I can't remember a time I didn't want to know God. I begged my parents to take me to church, and they faithfully dropped me off each Sunday. I began counting on myself to refrain from the bad things and pursued doing the good things. However, the one thing I wasn't counting on was sin. Looking back, I believe I had just been religiously house trained.

When I was a teen, my world changed in a single day. Dad's picture was on the front page of the local newspaper. He had been asked to resign from his very public position. The newspaper article spared his hidden lifestyle: alcoholism. The public humiliation escalated his addiction. He was intoxicated every day. We had to move out of town, and our family fell into extremely difficult times. Dad couldn't keep a job so Mom went to work for the first time in her life. My brother and I got part-time jobs after school and handed the folks our paychecks.

This pattern continued until my dad decided to throw in the towel. He chose of all days the day of my high school graduation. Mom was awakened early in the morning by a phone call from Western Union. They read her a message from my dad. Essentially he said he was a failure and couldn't stop drinking. He planned to take his life so we would get the insurance money. We had no idea where he was.

I went to graduation alone and cried through the whole thing.

In the days that followed we waited to hear of his fate. Days turned into a week, Mom turned into a wreck, and I turned to my high school sweetheart for solace. One night in a vulnerable moment, we fell into each other's arms and—well—you know the rest of the story.

A few weeks later Dad showed up. He'd been on a binge down in Mexico. We were relieved he was OK, but my plans for a brighter future were about to end.

Damaged Goods

A month later I learned I was pregnant. I was seventeen, unmarried, destitute, and pregnant! My home-grown theology assured me that I was damaged goods. I questioned God and blamed my dad.

"Why did you let this happen to me God? I've tried to be a good girl while many of my classmates flaunted their immoral lifestyle. If Dad hadn't left us, I wouldn't have made this mistake. Now I'm the one who is being punished. I have to give up all my dreams." I cried as I pounded my pillow without understanding.

Looking back I can see that my religious zeal as a young girl was just that—religious zeal! Inside I was actually dead in my trespasses and sins.

I reluctantly married my boyfriend. After the grim, meaningless ceremony and dinner with our parents, we drove to our furnished studio apartment near the university. It was complete with hot- and cold-running roaches.

My husband went to college on a full scholarship, and I went to work as a secretary. Within a few months our son arrived, and we were instantly in love! But the constant financial strain left little room for anything but survival. We lived under a gigantic cloud of lost dreams. We were weighed down by our circumstances, but we pressed on for the magic ticket: a college degree. It promised a rosy future. After college my husband took that ticket and headed out of town. The note he left told me that he had to get away and find himself. I wanted to get away and find him, too, but for reasons closely associated with murder.

I felt betrayed and abandoned once again. I figured God was punishing me because I got pregnant before marriage. Two days later that feeling deepened when I found out I was expecting another baby. I had to move home with my parents, and I hated my life.

Right before our beautiful daughter was born, my husband and I reconciled. He was so humble, broken, and weighed down with guilt. He wanted to make our marriage work. I did, too, but I was wickedly sanctimonious. I thought he should do some kind of penance. I wanted him to hurt as much as he'd hurt me. Our home wasn't a very happy one. The cycle of pain and guilt continued, and it looked as though nothing would break it.

Then a couple of years later, a movement hit America like a tidal wave. It promised women relief and liberation from their unhappy marriages. I sat up and listened. I needed relief, and I needed someone to blame for all my misery. *Ah ha,* I thought, *it's my husband! I knew it all along.* Before I could liberate myself, God intervened.

God Has to Change Us

Someone once said, "God has to change us before we can change the world—one person at a time." That quote became real to me in the 1960s when God changed my world through one person. It was the beginning of the Jesus Movement! It started at UCLA and was spreading across America like a prairie fire. A man named Bill Bright had written a tiny evangelical tract called *The Four Spiritual Laws.* The plan of salvation was written within the pages of this tiny booklet, and God used it to bring the last great revival in America.

My friend Harriet stopped by with one of those tracts in her purse. She later told me that her heart was pounding out of her chest. She knew the answer to all the problems in my life was Jesus. After we sat down for a cup of coffee, she asked if she could share something with me. I nodded.

She began reading me from this little booklet, "Did you know that God loves you and has a wonderful plan for your life?"

I started to weep. By the time she reached the end of the tract, I prayed and received Christ as my Savior. It was the most important day of my life.

Mutual Change

Three months later, my husband received Christ. It was a new beginning in our lives and our marriage. I'd like to tell you we've lived happily ever after, but that isn't supported in Scripture; it's from fairy tales. My husband and I are still married, and he's the love of my life. The love we have is different than before. It's God's love. It's his power that has changed us, but we had to learn that conversion was indeed just a beginning.

The Christian life is all about change. It's a lifelong process called *sanctification*. Through this process God changes us from one degree of glory to the next. And when God changes a life, it is unmistakable just as Pastor James MacDonald says, "If our faith hasn't changed us, then it hasn't saved us."

Since my conversion, God has used our once-rocky marriage as a platform to minister to other women going through similar circumstances. If they don't know Christ, this is always the starting point of counseling them. The foundation of this is John 15:5, which says apart from God, we can do nothing.

Looking Back and Seeing God

Now when I look back at our early marriage—and the rest of my life for that matter, I can see God's hand. I'm convinced that's the only time we should look back. I'm sure when the Apostle Paul looked back at his life, he could see it, too. Before he came to Christ, he was determined to persecute Christians, and he was intent on doing huge damaged to the church (Acts 9). But as he was traveling on the road to Damascus, the Lord turned the tables on Paul. He met him there and spoke to him directly. Paul gave his life to Christ as a result of that experience and lived out the rest of his days for the Lord. When you read the account of Paul's life, you see that he didn't settle down to live a comfy life. Paul's life was filled with trials and tribulation, all for the glory of God and the furtherance of the gospel.

Attention Getters

Now God got Paul's attention on the road to Damacus, and it began a journey filled with not only trials and tribulations but blessings and joy. Remember not all change is difficult. Sometimes change is accomplished through blessings because God loves to bless his children's lives. However, he knows that if all we have in life are blessings, we might respond to change with ambivalence and live the Christian life on cruise control as ho-hum sightseers on a journey toward heaven! The tool God often uses as an attention getter is pain, including emotional pain. Pain isn't meant to devalue us; God simply wants to get us to a place where we are ready to listen. His desire is to take our self-willed disposition and turn us into Holy Spirit-controlled believers through whom he works his will. Our pain then becomes a platform for him to display his glory.

A Second Chance

At the time, I wasn't eager for the spot on my lung to become that kind of platform for God to do his work. After I had learned I might be facing cancer, my faith was put to the test. I'd taken my good health for granted. The thing that frightened me the most wasn't the thought of having cancer—it was the biopsy. All I could imagine was this ghastly javelin-sized needle being thrust through my chest and into my lung.

The next week a high definition CT scan was scheduled before the tortuous procedure. We drove to the hospital in the wee hours of the morning. I knew our friends and family were praying. As I stared out the car window, I began planning my funeral. I tried to visualize the face of my soon-to-be widowed husband's new wife.

When we arrived at the hospital, it was still dark. The halls were empty and eerie. After a long wait, someone called me into a tiny cubicle for some blood tests. Then, they hooked up some gizmo into my hand to administer medication and hopefully some miracle juice to calm me for the biopsy. While waiting for the high definition CT scan, I started thinking of all the widows who would show up after my funeral with casseroles and cakes for my husband.

After the scan, we waited. Within a few minutes the radiologist came out with a grin on his face.

"We don't have to do a biopsy. You have an inverted artery in your lung. It's nothing to ever concern you. A new artery simply spun off another, flipped over, and looked like a tadpole on the X-ray. It's a common thing. Go out to breakfast and celebrate the goodness of God!"

I hugged the doctor. My future was intact for the moment. I called as many folks as I could to share the good news. Unbeknownst to me, the word had gotten out through emails, and it spread across the country. Their prayers and how God was glorified through them humbled me.

That day I was spared from imminent death from cancer, but the truth is it was just a reprieve. Someday I will die. Statistics prove it's 100 percent guaranteed. I don't have any fear of death, but the process getting there can seem a bit daunting. I know I will be in heaven with my Lord and Savior, but I won't be there because of anything I did. I will be there because of what Jesus did. He died for my sins. I will be there because of that very important day when I received him as my Lord and Savior.

Do You Remember the Day?

Do you remember the day you became a new creation in Christ? I'm not talking about religion. Dump religion; it's about a personal relationship with Jesus Christ. Without him all the changes you are going through will seem cruel and unfair. Life will be more like boot camp if you don't know him. Remember Jesus had you in mind when he died on the cross. He paid for your sin because it was a part of his plan.

Your part is simple but profound. If you've never received his free gift of eternal life, make this your moment to kneel before him. This is one prayer to which God never says no. When we ask him to give us eternal life because we believe in his Son, he always says, "Yes." Kneel before him with a believing heart and pray:

> Lord, I understand that you died on the cross because you love me and want to give me eternal life. I am persuaded that your Father sent you to rescue me from my sin. I believe that you died for my sin and rose. I trust you to give me eternal life. I confess that you are the resurrection and the life and that all who believe in you will never die. I believe this. Thank you, Father in heaven, for your free gift of eternal life. In his name, amen.

This new beginning is the front end of change! After conversion, life is nothing *but* change.

I had a wild and crazy friend whose life was also nothing but change. In fact she was obsessed with it, but the changes were *external*. I am learning that God is far more interested in *internal* change, the kind that takes place in the heart. Maybe you will identify with her struggle.

Notes:

1. Joni Eareckson, *Joni* (Grand Rapids, MI Zondervan 25 av 2001) 5
2. Bill Bright, *The Four Spiritual Laws* (Orlando Florida, Campus Crusade for Christ 1960)
3. Ed Underwood, *When God Breaks Your Heart,* (Colorado Springs, Co. Cook Publishing 2008) 113

TWO

Extreme Change

---

*"I consider that our present sufferings
are not worth comparing with the glory
that will be revealed in us."*
Romans 8:18

Our culture is obsessed with change, but most of the changes are external: a nip here, a tuck there, new teeth, changes of hair color, makeup, and even permanent eyeliner. There is a surgery for everything from facelifts to breast implants, and liposuction for weight loss. Most of these procedures need constant maintenance.

However, the kind of change God is into is internal and eternal. He wants to transform us from within. The word *transformation* in the original language means "makeover." God wants to makeover our hearts. The process is usually polar opposite of what we pictured.

External Makeovers

I had a friend Monica who was obsessed with external makeovers. She tried every new diet that came along. She was always touting a new theory for staying as skinny as a flagpole. Exercise became an obsession.

One day her best friend dropped by to visit and knocked on Monica's door.

"Come in!" she hollered from the kitchen, huffing and puffing.

Julie entered the house and heard this loud, rhythmic, clunking noise. When she rounded the corner, Monica was wearing her ski boots and running in place to get aerobic! Along with exercise, health foods and vitamin supplements became part of her regimen.

Monica admitted to me much later on that she'd always been obsessive-compulsive. Even as a child she was driven and lived for the next conquest. By college she had her life all mapped out. After college she married a handsome military officer in a beautiful wedding ceremony, complete with soldiers holding the crossed swords as they exited the chapel. A few years later, children arrived.

Soon they bought a home for their expanding family, and Monica got right down to the business of changing it. She'd flip through all the latest decorator magazines, fabric samples, wallpaper books, and paint samples for ideas. She hired folks to do the projects, and it all came together as quickly as the money left her bank account.

Eventually she drifted into the era of self-examination. She decided to seek advice from a counselor, a decision that lasted nearly twenty years. She was convinced she could figure out the mystery of iniquity. *Why did my mom do this?* she asked. *Why didn't my dad do that?* Her focus left her with a lot more questions than answers.

Then she turned back to music. She'd taken years of piano as a child and then left it for something else. When she took it up again, she learned how to improvise. If you wanted to hear "Amazing Grace" played like a polka, she'd bang it out in nothing flat.

Then, she returned to her first love; painting. In time more than seven hundred sketches and paintings filled the walls and lined the closets. (I confess every time I was around her I felt like a gigantic slug.)

We moved out of state and lost touch. When we were transferred back, I heard she'd gone to work at a local university teaching art, but our paths never crossed.

Several years later a friend of mine called to tell me Monica had cancer.

"It's cancer of the bone marrow. It's horrible. She's in the hospital, and they are going to do a bone marrow transplant."

I was stunned. Monica had taken better care of herself than any person who lived on the planet, including octogenarian Jack LaLanne. I called her immediately. She sounded extremely weak, and I hardly recognized her voice.

"Judy, it's good to hear from you. I've missed you. The doctors told me if my bone marrow transplant is successful, I have a very good chance of living several more years. Please pray it works."

I assured her I'd be praying.

We got the news: it didn't work.

"What's the next step?" I asked her, hoping for a miracle.

"I go on a regimen of chemotherapy and other cancer-blasting drugs. They hope this will slow down the disease."

Days turned into weeks, weeks turned into months, and Monica turned her attention to medical websites for the latest research on a cure for her disease. She chased her cancer with a vengeance. Admittedly, ignorance isn't bliss, but her research provided her with more fear than anything else.

Meeting God at a Dead End

One day Monica seemed to hit the wall. She'd come to a dead end. Worn out and discouraged, she'd lost hope. She'd finally come to a place where the difficulties became so bad she'd reached her limit. She tried everything and exhausted all her options.

The uncertainty of her future got her thinking about the Lord and her relationship with him. Sometimes it takes a miraculous rescue/touch from God to break out of simply going through the motions of the Christian life. She realized that what she'd been doing wasn't working.

That's why God has to bring us low so we'll listen and then he can lift us up. Yes, his plan can be very difficult, but his love never fails. In the end it's always the best plan because it is eternal. Monica's agony and fear turned her heart toward him. She cried out and asked him to help her. The paradox is that God is the one who pursues us first. A. W. Tozer says, "We pursue God because, and only because, he has first put an urge within us that spurs us to the pursuit."

Like every other task Monica faced, she began her pursuit with a vengeance. She started a feeding frenzy in God's word. She purchased commentaries, Bible dictionaries, Word Study books, classical devotionals, and a topical Bible. She started spending hours on end studying and absorbing this new banquet cuisine.

In the past Monica, like so many of us, built her faith on what other people said. Now, she was receiving Holy Spirit-powered transformation. The Lord was bringing her to a whole new understanding of his power dwelling within her (Eph. 3:17–19; Gal. 2:20).

Moment by moment and step by step, God was changing her perspective on her illness and even its purpose. He was calling her to display his glory through a vehicle called cancer. She told me later that she began to see the sovereignty of God throughout Scripture, understanding that God, who created her and all that is in the universe, does as he pleases (Ps. 115:3). These truths became an anchor to her faith because faith comes from God (Rom. 10:17). In fact, without faith it is impossible to please God (Heb. 11:6). She told me she stopped focusing on a cure and started focusing on doing his will, which brought her peace. A. W. Tozer helped her come to this decision:

> Let a man set his heart only on doing the will of God and he is instantly free. If we understand our first and sole duty is to consist of loving God supremely and loving everyone, even our enemies, for God's dear sake, then we can enjoy spiritual tranquility under every circumstance.

Monica shared what a privilege it was to be given her light and momentary trouble, knowing that is was achieving for her an eternal glory that outweighed them all (2 Cor. 4:17). She had begun to always quote Scripture as she talked. I loved that about her.

Family Ties

When we get right with God, it affects relationships. Monica's relationships with her extended family began to change. All the petty stuff didn't matter anymore. She reconciled with distant relatives she hadn't talked to in years. She had no problem asking for forgiveness for anything and everything she could have done to cause problems.

The sweetest change was her love for her husband. She told me her illness brought about a closeness she'd always dreamed about. She no longer needed to be right about everything.

Her humility calmed the troubled waters with her adult children. Daily phone calls and visits became the norm. She was able to savor and enjoy her grandchildren. She was slowly developing an eternal perspective about everything in life.

As time went by, I found myself wanting to spend more time with her. Her passionate pursuit of God captivated me. Her peace and tranquility in the midst of uncertainty and shattered dreams challenged me. I marveled at her unmistakable joy. Larry Crabb explains what shattered dreams accomplish:

> "Shattered dreams open the door to better dreams that we do not properly value until the dreams that we improperly value are changed. Shattered dreams destroy false expectations, such as the "victorious Christian life with no real struggle or failure." They help us discover true hope. We need the help of shattered dreams to put us in touch with what we must long for, to create a heart-felt appetite for better dreams. And living for the better

dreams generates a new, unfamiliar feeling that we eventually recognize as joy."

An Amazing Gift

"Judy, did you know that God has given me a great gift?" she told me on the phone one day.

"Really? What is it?"

"It's cancer. Cancer has been an amazing tool that has gotten my attention. Up until now my life has been a long series of busyness, noise, commotion, and discontent. He's taken my self-seeking heart and latched it on to his. He's doing more than I could have ever asked."

People asked Monica how they could get the same kind of joy and peace she had. Her response revealed the secret to living the Christian life.

"You don't have to get anything; you just have to tap into what Christ has already given to you as a believer."

"How do you do that?" I asked.

"You give up the right to run your life! Judy, the day I told the Lord I couldn't do this thing called cancer anymore was the day he began to transform me. He never intended me to live the Christian life in my own power. That's religion. He came to live his life through me. The day I surrendered my life, he took over. His power is what is getting me through all this."

Judy, sometimes it takes years, but eventually you discover that the greatest hindrance to God's blessing in your life is not others, it is yourself; your self-will, stubborn pride, and personal ambition. You cannot fulfill God's purposes for your life while focusing on your own plans.

As time passed Monica spent copious amounts of time in waiting rooms, laboratories, X-ray rooms, or hospital beds dealing with all the side affects from her illness. She called these venues her "mission field." When she wasn't doing mission work in the hospital or doctor's offices, she was a missionary in a cancer support group. She told me she wasn't interested in getting support; she wanted to lend it.

"When I first started going to the meetings, the atmosphere was pessimistic and depressing," she told me. "Most of the folks were there to learn the latest research, find a new treatment, or receive pity for their suffering. All I wanted to do was help them focus on God and what he can do. I stood up one night and told them what God was doing in my life. I shared how they could know him personally and how he'd given me peace and purpose with an uncertain future. Judy, God is using my cancer to spread the gospel.

"'He wants to carry your burdens,' I told the audience one night as I taught from the Scriptures. 'He wants to make a difference in your life. Don't waste this disease. Imagine if you lived your entire life healthy but spent eternity apart from God? Thank him that cancer has opened your eyes to your need for him. Faith isn't figuring out how God will change things; it is the knowledge that he will bring his will into being. Never judge God by suffering, judge suffering by the cross.'"

Monica's circle of influence grew through emails. Her gifted writing was shared over the Internet. People forwarded them around the world. Missionaries were gleaning hope and healing for their own challenges. Recipients were gaining insight and encouragement, by reading firsthand of his transforming power in the midst of a terminal disease. I looked forward to every one of them. She was asked to share what she was learning from the pulpit of her church.

Her pastor wanted people to catch the difference Christ makes when living with a catastrophic disease.

Reality Check

After looking at Monica's story when you face difficult changes and challenges in your own life, what is your source of comfort? Have your circumstances forced you to examine your own faith? Have you asked yourself, *Why am I going through this?* Are you searching for answers? Are you desperate enough to cry out to God like Monica did? Remember he is the only one who can make something beautiful out of all the confusion. He has a plan, and it may be different than yours, but his plan is better, and it's eternal.

God's Plan for Mary and Martha

When I think of people in Scripture who, through an illness like Monica's, were used to reveal God's plan, I think of Lazarus and his sisters, Martha and Mary.

In John 11 Lazarus and his sisters were close friends of Jesus. When Lazarus became ill, his sisters sent word to Jesus in another town. Because his condition was so grave, they naturally assumed he would run right over to help. After all, he was their friend and friends help others in their time of need. When Jesus got the news though, he decided to stay where he was for two more days. He told his disciples that this sickness wouldn't end in death. It would be an opportunity for his power and glory to be displayed.

Do you think Mary and Martha were a bit miffed by his delay? Being a woman, I have a feeling they were. I imagine they were thinking, *Gee, you'd think Jesus would drop everything to come and help a friend. After all, he opened the eyes of a blind man. Can't he come and save our brother?* But Mary and Martha didn't see the bigger picture. They had no idea Jesus was God incarnate. Jesus wasn't only going to teach them about his perfect timing but show them something about himself they didn't know.

When Jesus finally showed up, he went with Mary and Martha to the place where Lazarus was buried. They protested about his entering the tomb by saying that the stench in the cave would be dreadful. They think Lazarus's story is done and buried, but Jesus knows that his two-day delay hasn't changed anything.

"Didn't I tell you that you would see God's glory if you only believed?"

God's glory unfolded as they rolled away the stone in front of the cave, and Jesus prayed, "Father, thank you for hearing me. You always hear me, but I said it out loud for the sake of all these people standing here, so they will believe you sent me." Then, he shouted, "Lazarus, come out!"

Lazarus came out, wrapped in grave cloths. His face was still covered in a head cloth. Jesus told them to take off the head wrap.

That day Jesus showed Lazarus, Mary, Martha, and hundreds who had come to his funeral, that he is the resurrection and the life. Had he come earlier, people would have argued whether he had even performed a miracle.

Out of Options

Monica's doctor and her family encouraged her to make one more attempt at a bone marrow transplant, and she was hoping for a miracle. A few days before she was supposed to enter the hospital for all the grueling preparations, the procedure was called off. Her cancer was out of control, and she was out of options. The next day she sent out this email:

"At the last minute, the Lord stepped in and said, 'No, this is not my will for you now!'

"How could I question this? God's timing is always perfect. It is the regrouping through this fork in the road that has become my problem.

"All I could say was, 'Huh?' I knew this was God's providential will, and I could accept that, but what about my battered emotions, all the preparation that went into preparing for four to six weeks in the hospital and then at home unable to go anywhere for a total of one hundred days? Now what?

"The peace the Lord had previously given me slipped away as my humanness took hold. My mind was filled with questions about my limited options and future treatment. First of all, I am human, and the turn of events would cause anyone to falter. I guess secretly I had hoped that God would heal the cancer. I had hoped for a longer life through this bone marrow transplant. But God had another plan, a better plan, one designed by him alone.

"During this process, I became filled with gratitude for the gift of the death of God's Son to save us from our sin. God's timing in the crucifixion was perfect. It did not seem so to the apostles. He bore the horrible pain of the cross—the perfect one, the God–Man. He did this so all of mankind could have forgiveness of sin, eternal life, and fullness of life here on earth regardless of our circumstances.

"Before he faced the cross, Jesus prayed in Luke 22:42, "'Father if you are willing, remove this cup from me, yet not my will, but yours be done." Now an angel of the Lord appeared to him, strengthening him. And being in agony, he was praying very fervently, his sweat became like drops of blood, falling down upon the ground.' In the end Jesus suffers the pain of the cross and says, 'Father, into your hands I commit my Spirit.' He abandoned himself to the will of the Father.

"How could all this relate to me in my situation? I knew I needed to abandon my life to the will of God just as Christ did to his Father.

"One morning I awakened very early. I went into my family room and lit a fire. I made myself a cup of tea, settled into my cozy chair, and covered myself with my favorite blanket. As I began to read, I began to weep. I was overcome with emotion and a deep desire to surrender my life completely to God.

"I got down on the floor, prostrate before the fireplace, and I asked the Lord to minister to my heart. I waited for what seemed a very long time, and then it happened! The whispering breeze of his presence came over me into the kind of ruthless trust we all desire. I never wanted to leave this place of perfect peace. Jesus met me, and I knew my life was secure in whatever plans he held."

Monica's response to impending death displayed the grace of our long-suffering God and his glory to thousands who read that email; the folks in her cancer support group, the medical teams, and all her friends and family. They saw the difference Jesus Christ makes when one of his children is facing death.

The End of Death at the End

A few weeks after Monica abandoned herself to God, she stepped into his presence safely home. When Jesus raised Lazarus from the dead, it was his signal that there would be no more death at the end for those who belong to him. Monica's departure was just the end of her earthly story.

Nearly one thousand people packed the church at her memorial service. When the microphone was opened up for personal comments, one person after another stood to speak and share how God's glory shined through Monica's life:

- "Monica brought me from despair and discouragement to dependence on Jesus Christ. I found a peace I'd never known ... through him."
- "Monica called me during my darkest hours. Her words lifted my downcast soul when she prayed for me."
- "Monica's courage and faith affected my baby faith. I wanted what she had. Her enthusiasm gave me a hunger for God and the Bible."
- "I thought God was mad at me, and that's why I had cancer. Monica showed me how much God loved me and how he had gotten my attention through cancer. I discovered a whole new way of living and dying because Monica pointed me to him."
- "Monica taught me that this world is not our home. Heaven is where everything will turn out right."

Several weeks later with the testimonies of Monica's impact still fresh in my mind, I turned to Paul's words in 2 Corinthians during my personal quiet time:

We don't go around preaching about ourselves; we preach Christ Jesus, the Lord. All we say about ourselves is that we are your servants because of what Jesus has done for us (4:5, NIV).

For instance, we know that when these bodies of ours are taken down like tents and folded away, they will be replaced by resurrection bodies in heaven ... God-made, not handmade ... and we'll never have to relocate our "tents" again. Sometimes we can hardly wait to move ... and so we cry out in frustration. Compared to what's coming, living conditions around here seem like a stopover in an unfurnished shack, and we're tired of it! We've been given a glimpse of the real thing, our true home, and our resurrection bodies! (5:1–5, MSG)

I realized I had learned some valuable life lessons about from Monica's life. In the midst of terminal cancer, God had given her purpose. Like many of us, Monica sought life through the externals for years, but when her plans fell through they drew her to God. It is the way he works. He transformed her life and gave her peace and purpose in the midst of pain. Her suffering and loss functioned as a catalyst to transform others and display his glory.

She's in heaven now and finally has the body she'd always dreamed.

I find it a bit easier to see how cancer can bring about a dramatic life-change; change that displays God glory. But what about a person who falls into sin and dismantles an entire family? How can God bring Glory through that kind of a mess? Bonnie's story may surprise you.

Notes:

1. A. W. Tozer, The Pursuit of God (Camp Hill, PA Christian Publication 1982)11
2. Larry Crabb, Shattered Dreams,(Colorado Springs, CO. Waterbrook Press 2001)35
3. A.W.Tozer, Worldofquotes.com

THREE

Forgiveness Changes Everything

"I will restore to you the years
that the locust has eaten."
Joel 2:25

"The Lord will give grace and glory; no good thing
will he withhold from them that walk uprightly."
Psalm 84:11b

I sat across from a very petite, stylish woman named Bonnie on the first day of our Bible study. She was meek and quiet, yet something about her drew me to her. When called on to share her answer to one of the questions, her gentle voice spoke with wisdom and grace.

A few weeks later our class had an extended day and a luncheon. Bonnie offered to host it at her home. I made my way up many winding roads to reach it at the summit. The minute I saw it I knew we were in for a treat.

Stepping inside confirmed all my expectations. Her home was breathtaking, as was the view. Massive furnishings were lavish, yet tasteful and inviting. The same palette of colors flowed through each room.

Bonnie's kitchen was a cook's dream. It was very large and made us all feel welcome. She had all kinds of food in serving dishes and bowls. She had set out cold drinks by the pretty plates and napkins. We served ourselves and went into the dining room to begin our banquet.

One of the gals spoke up and said, "Bonnie, many of us don't know you very well, but we'd like to. Tell us a little bit about yourself and how you came to know Christ."

Bonnie swallowed hard. "Oh dear ... my story is really multicolored. Are you sure you want to hear it?"

Twenty heads whipped around toward Bonnie like flags in a hurricane.

"Yes!"

"Well, let's see. Guess I'll begin at the beginning. I grew up in a wonderful Christian home and I adored my parents. My dad was a wise man who gave us great counsel. We trusted his wisdom. I have nothing but fond memories of my childhood.

"After high school I went to the college my dad selected, and soon I met a nice man. No bells and whistles went off, but Dad said he was a fine young man, and I should marry him, so I did.

"Our marriage was compatible and steady. Soon children arrived, and we took them to church every week. When they went off to grade school, I began dabbling in interior design. I had never studied it formally, but folks told me I had good taste and innovative ideas."

(We all agreed as we looked around us at her home.)

"Soon I opened my own business at the height of Houston's building boom. I designed hundreds of model homes and decorated many of Houston's finest estates. My clientele were the rich and famous. I loved it. Business was astounding. As our kids entered high school, my work consumed me. By then our marriage was like an afterthought. My husband took care of everything on the homefront, including his own business, and I took care of mine. We passed like ships in the night.

"Temptation walked in the door of my design center in the form of Mr. Charm. He said he owned a company who manufactured fine furniture in England. I had purchased many items from his catalog but never met him. I was captivated by his British accent and his sudden interest in all the things I loved doing. He told me about his quaint English cottage in the countryside that was filled with antiques. He showed me pictures of his English garden. I was so impressed. We talked for hours on the phone, and within a short period of time, we began having an affair. He told me he loved me and wanted to marry me. I'm embarrassed to say that I accepted his proposal, put my business up for sale, made a truckload of money, sent my two older kids off to college, and filed for divorce."

Everyone at the table gasped. I am sure most of us were thinking, *What? You did what?* Like Clairee in the movie *Steel Magnolias*, we begged her to go on with all the juicy details.

"Within a few months we were off to London. When we arrived, I was shocked when I learned there was no quaint cottage in the country. He lived in a dingy apartment in the city. He gave me some song and dance about selling it. The day after we arrived he deposited all my money in his bank account and left town on a business trip.

"Obviously from that point on, everything in my life collapsed. I was alone all the time in a strange city. In my mind I was a scarlet woman who had left her children in the dust. To kill time, I began taking long walks. One day I stumbled upon a small mission's church right in the heart of London. Desperate, lonely, and afraid, I went inside. An older woman greeted me from behind her desk. Within minutes I found myself blurting out my woeful story to this perfect stranger. She listened intently and made no comments. When I finished, she got up, walked around her desk, and hugged me.

"'Could you come back this evening for our Bible study? We serve dinner and then we pray. Let us help you.' I couldn't believe it when I told her I'd come.

"Over time this wonderful church wrapped their arms around me and ministered to me. I'll never forget the day I wept, repented of my sin, asked God to forgive me, and received him as Lord.

"I had hoped the situation with Mr. Charm would change, but it never did. Several months later I moved back to the States to the back bedroom of my sister's home in Virginia. I'd lost everything: my family, my money, and my reputation. I knew God had forgiven me, but I couldn't forgive myself." Bonnie's vulnerability touched our hearts, evidenced by tears spilling down some cheeks, including mine.

Deception Is Always Knocking

Someone once said when we are deceived, we don't know it, and that was exactly what had happened to Bonnie. It could just as easily have happened to you or me.

Have you ever been deceived? Have you ever made so many poor choices that your self-loathing has convinced you to give up on yourself? Well, you aren't the first and you won't be the last. In fact, a very prominent man in the

New Testament fell victim to this trap as well. His name is Peter.

Peter and his brother, Andrew, were fishermen when Jesus called them both to become fishers of men. In Mark 1:17 when Jesus said, "Come, follow me," Peter left behind his nets and followed him. Peter was a very impulsive guy. He shot from the hip. (I like that about Peter. He and I are a lot alike.) But remember the reason Jesus picked the disciples wasn't because they were so special. Jesus chose people he would change and then use for his purposes.

Peter became the recognized leader of these men. He was in an inner circle of three, but he often spoke without thinking. He was brash but enthusiastic and passionate. After the Last Supper Jesus told the disciples they would all deny him. Peter took Jesus on and insisted he would never do that. Jesus went on to say, "Tonight before the rooster crows, twice you will disown me three times." Peter argued with Jesus and vowed he would not only die with him, but he'd never disown his Lord.

When Jesus was arrested in Gethsemane, Peter cut off the ear of one of the guards to stop him. Then, they all ran out of fear. Later in a courtyard, when accused of being one who had been with Jesus, Peter denied it. By the time the rooster crowed twice, Peter had denied Jesus three times. Imagine the regret and guilt as he recalled all the memories he had of seeing him heal the sick, raise the dead, walk on water, and feed the multitudes. He hated himself for what he had done.

After Peter witnessed Christ's crucifixion, resurrection, and re-appearance to the disciples, he and some of the disciples decided to go back to fishing. (John 21: 2) Picture Peter, the downcast soul, with a cloud of shame following him night and day. The disciples got in their boat, fished all night, and caught nothing. When the sun came up, Jesus, in another post-resurrection appearance, was standing on the beach, but they didn't recognize him.

"Good morning! Did you catching anything?" Jesus asked.

"No," they answered.

He told them to throw their net off the right side of the boat. They did, and all of a sudden there were so many fish in it that they weren't strong enough to pull in the net.

"It's Jesus!" John said to Peter.

Peter's reacted by diving into the sea and swimming for the shore. The disciples followed in their boat.

As Peter ran toward Jesus, Jesus stood still and pointed his finger at Peter screaming, "Get away from me you big loser. I'm done with you. You can't be trusted. I can't use traitors like you. I'll never forget what you did to me."

Is that was Jesus said?

No!

That's what I would have said to someone who had hurt me and never owned up to it! It was what Bonnie would have said to herself.

You see, part of our humanity wants revenge or simply doesn't understand the depth of God's grace. I confess that at one time I felt the need not only to earn his forgiveness but to expect it of others. I've sentenced myself to punishment in a jail of my own making. I've felt unworthy of forgiveness. How about you?

Yet Jesus always forgives. If we confess our sins, he's faithful and just to forgive and cleanse us of all our unrighteousness (1 John 1:9). It's Satan who whispers lies into our thoughts that we must atone for our sin. He, not God, keeps a record of wrongs against us.

Back to the reunion of Jesus with Peter on the beach, the truth is Jesus asked Peter three times, "Do you love me?" And Peter told Jesus three times of his love, once for each of the three times he denied Jesus. Jesus wasn't as interested in Peter's words as much as he was Peter's heart. Peter had a repentant heart, and it's better to be a follower who fails than one who fails to follow.

That failure allowed Jesus to give Peter the power to become one of the greatest saints of the faith. Peter realized that he was just the vessel:

But we have this treasure in jars of clay to show that this all-surpassing power is from God and not from us. (2 Cor. 4:7, NIV)

His grace makes all the difference in our lives when we have blown it. Let yourself off the hook. Repent and ask for forgiveness. God's got some amazing plans to work through you, an ordinary, flawed, fully forgiven clay vessel.

A New Beginning

Like Peter, Bonnie started over. God is the God of second chances. She made enough money decorating model homes in a neighborhood near her sister's so she could move to California. She wanted to be near her kids who were in college. She desperately wanted to mend their relationships and ask forgiveness for all the pain she'd caused. She was humble and contrite. Her children offered her grace and forgiveness.

She went to work for an Oriental rug merchant. Soon she was selling more rugs than the owner because the customers loved how she helped them choose the right rug. She'd go to their homes and help with other decorating ideas. Soon she found herself in business again. It was during this time that Bonnie met a woman who had a powerful ministry to other women (some homeless), whose lives had been destroyed by sin and Satan's captivity. She was so impressed at this grace-based ministry that she got involved. She made a decision to tithe 95 percent of her earnings to help change lives. It's a discipline she does to this day because as she says, "You cannot out-give God. He owns it all!"

God continued to work not only in Bonnie's bold giving but in her heart as well. One day, one of the street women had to be hospitalized, and Bonnie went with her to the hospital. Once Bonnie got her settled in her room, she was curious about a curtain completely drawn around the next bed. The muffled sobs coming from behind it touched her heart. Finally, she stepped through the curtain to offer help. A woman lay terminally ill, and her husband was in anguish and tears. She shared the gospel with both of them, and they received Christ.

A Second Chance at Love

Months later Bonnie got a call from the husband whom she had met in the hospital. He'd hunted her down. His wife had died shortly after the hospital visit, and he wanted to thank her. He asked her to have dinner with him. Today—years later—they are happily married. He also happened to be a builder, and Bonnie just happens to use her gift of design to help him.

The God of second chances restored her to being a happy, contented wife and mother to a loving family. Today, his glory is being displayed through her life to other women who have hit rock bottom. When she looks back, Bonnie cherishes the grace God has shown her—even when she walked further from him. She encourages others in similar situations to reach out and receive what God freely gives.

That offer extends to you as well. Won't you receive it?

Let the Past Be the Past

There is also a flip side to Bonnie's story of grace and restoration. Not only did she have to forgive herself, but her family had to forgive her before they could find healing.

Anger and resentment can stifle the work God is doing in you and blind you to the true purpose behind the pain. Do you need to forgive someone else? Maybe it is family member who lied, a boss who fired you, someone who borrowed money and never paid it back, a spouse who cheated on you, a friend who ruined your reputation through gossip, or a parent who abandoned you?

As painful as it is until you forgive the offender, you will not see how God is going to use that situation in your life. He loves to turn crucifixion into resurrection. He wants to display his power and his splendor through your life. Just as Genesis 50:20 says, "You intended to harm me, but God intended it for good to accomplish what is now being done, the saving of many lives." (NIV)

Now remember, forgiveness doesn't necessarily mean reconciliation. Reconciliation is between two parties who agree and own their own sin. For example, consider the woman whose husband abuses her and never admits it? It would be foolish to go back to that. We can fully forgive another person, but that doesn't guarantee reconciliation. A relationship takes two. Forgiving our enemies frees us to get on with our lives.

If we claim that we're free of sin, we're only fooling ourselves. A claim like that is errant nonsense. On the other hand, if we admit our sins—make a clean breast of them—He won't let us down; He'll be true to himself. He'll forgive our sins and purge us of all wrongdoing. If we claim that we've never sinned, we out-and-out contradict God—make a liar out of Him. A claim like that only shows off our ignorance of God. (1 John 1:8–10, MSG)

Forgiveness obtained through God's grace results in a new beginning that glorifies God. But what if events bring death to thousands of people at the hands of evil doers? What if entire cities are destroyed and lives are lost through a natural disaster? What then?

FOUR

A Change in the Landscape

"And the Lord will deliver me from every evil work
and preserve me for His heavenly kingdom.
To Him be glory forever and ever. Amen!"
2 Timothy 4:18

I am an early riser. It's not a virtue; it's my aches and pains. They have become my new alarm clock. I love going downstairs in the wee hours, making a pot of coffee, smelling its alluring aroma, slipping into my big easy chair, and savoring that first sip. It's my favorite time of day.

One morning seemed exceptionally quiet. I could hear faint singing from early birds in the distance, welcoming the dawn. Suddenly, the phone rang and startled me out of my serenity. *It's six forty-five in the morning! Who calls this early?*

Before I could greet the caller, my daughter blurted out, "Turn on the TV. A plane just flew into one of the towers of the World Trade Center."

"Oh my gosh, what is going on?" I asked as I grabbed the remote.

I watched the television for a few minutes and then with the phone in hand, made a mad dash up the stairs to wake up my husband.

"Honey, something horrible has happened. A plane just flew into the World Trade Center. They think it's an accident."

My husband grabbed his robe and made his way to the family room. Like many Americans we were mesmerized by what was unfolding. Suddenly another plane came into view. We gasped in wide-eyed horror as it flew, like a guided missile, into the second tower.

That day our country was attacked by terrorists. The grim reality was that the USA was no longer immune from war on her own soil. It changed the history books, that's for sure. But as the days and weeks past, God used this catastrophe to get folk's attention so he could change them.

One of those people was a young man named Lance. His mother Kathy is a dear friend. She and her husband lived through years of heartache over Lance's bad choices. They tried everything to help him get on with his life. In the end nothing changed long term. But on 9/11 Lance was about to get some help from heaven. He was alone in his dreary, darkened apartment watching all the coverage on TV. Even though he was hung-over from a bender the night before, the gut-wrenching reality of the attacks and the death of innocent lives got his attention. He thought about his own life and the years wasted on drugs and reckless living. The more he saw reruns of the imploding twin towers, he knew his own life was doing the same thing. He started to weep over his trashed life, his endless sin and all the pain he'd caused many innocent people. He tumbled off the couch, onto the floor and sobbed throughout the day and into the night. Like Jacob wrestling with God, he became exhausted and finally gave up in the wee hours of the morning. He cried out to God in repentance and begged Him to save His life. 9/11 was a very important day indeed.

Lance had been estranged from his parents for months and he wanted to tell them the good news. He found out they were away at their cabin. So he got cleaned up, he gassed up his car and headed up to the mountains. Imagine their surprise when they saw him coming up the long road to their cabin? They went out on their porch as Lance was getting out of his car.

"What's goin' on?" Kathy asked.

"I came to tell you that I gave my life to Christ this morning. The attacks opened my eyes to the empty life I've been living and I asked God to forgive me and save me and He did." He started to cry.

There was a lot of rejoicing that day. It was a new beginning. Since that time his life has gone in a new direction. Lance got into a faith-based recovery program, got a job with a future and a steady paycheck. He has never returned to the life he once knew. God used the affects of 9/11 to redirect this young man's desperate life.

New Life from the Ashes

Years later I met a woman who experienced the same kind of life-change from 9/11 as Lance. She shared her story at a conference I was speaking for. She didn't watch the attacks on television because she happened to be in one of the twin towers when the first plane hit!

"I worked in the North Tower of the World Trade Center. I was on the 102nd floor when the first plane hit the South

Tower. I saw it fly by my window in my peripheral vision, not really knowing what it was. Within seconds it exploded, and our building shook violently. Along with many colleagues, I headed to the stairs and started descending as fast as my feet could navigate them. When we made it to the 71st floor the second plane hit our building, but it was several floors above our escape route. Despite the pungent odor of jet fuel, the heat, the extreme rocking and vibrating of the building, we continued our racing descent. Chaos reined. My heart was pounding so hard it was difficult to breathe, but I finally made it to the first floor and ran outside.

"I was so exhausted I didn't think I had enough energy to leave the area, but the loud thumping noises shook me back to reality. The thumping was bodies hitting the ground like meteors. People jumping out of windows to escape the fire and smoke.

"After that fateful day, I had nightmares and panic attacks six and seven times daily. The post traumatic stress was paralyzing. I was deteriorating physically as well as mentally. After one year of therapy I decided I had to leave New York so I could get on with my life. I moved across country but the memories and problems continued to haunt me day and night.

"I had to go back to work and make a living, but fear was my constant companion. My thoughts took me back to the months before 9/11 when I began a spiritual journey for truth. Now my questions about God heightened along with all my fears.

"One day a co-worker invited me to attend her church. I had lots of questions for God and figured I might get some answers at her church so I accepted her invitation. The next Sunday I heard the Gospel for the first time in my life. When the Pastor gave an invitation, I found myself walking down the isle. I prayed and received him as my Lord and Savior and my life began to change. He became my strong tower, my refuge, my peace and joy.

"By the way" she said as she closed her message. "I have never had a panic attack or a nightmare since. Jesus set me free!"

Disasters get our attention and remind us of the brevity of life, don't they? But often they point us to a new way of living. I would be reminded of this once again, a few years later watching another early morning TV news show.

Gone with the Wind

Fast forward to 2005, when the United States was hit again by another inconceivable disaster, a natural one. We saw all the warnings on The Weather Channel, but no one could have prepared us for the kind of devastation that Hurricane Katrina would exact.

I will never forget waking up in the wee hours of the morning after she hit. I turned on the television and gasped as I watched in horror at what was being shown. I groaned at what the folks in Louisiana and Mississippi were experiencing. The devastation seemed beyond human comprehension. Some said it was like a half-tsunami/half-tornado that wouldn't quit. The suffering of the innocent seemed unfair. Nancy Guthrie explained it like this:

> Often when unfair, undeserved suffering comes into our lives, we demand to hold someone respon-sible ... the doctor who made a drastic error in judgment, the driver who had too much to drink, and the divorce lawyer who drove such a tough bargain. But the "someone" we hold responsible

for the suffering in this world is God. When we see deadly tsunamis, hurricanes, and earthquakes around the world, we can't help but wonder, God, are you still on the throne? As terrorism increases and the ozone layer decreases, as world economics rise and fall, we strain to keep believing that God is still on the throne. The writer of Hebrews assures us. "Your throne, O God, will last forever and ever, and righteousness will be the scepter of your kingdom." (Heb. 1:8)

My thoughts immediately went out to our dear friends Lois and Doug, who live in Biloxi. I had visited them just a few years before when I was at a conference in their area. Their home wasn't right on the coast but very close. My imagination took over, and I began to wonder what they were going through at that very moment. I was sure they'd lost everything, and I stopped and prayed for them.

In the days that followed I searched the Internet and found a website set up by their son-in-law in Tennessee that said Doug and Lois were safe and sound. I quickly wrote them an email.

Later she called me.

"We are so grateful to be alive..." Her words faded as silent sobs and deep emotions took over.

"The whole experience was life altering, Judy. There are so many losses and so much devastation!"

The Surge Takes Its Toll

A few months later we received their annual Christmas letter. Doug gave us a lot more details of their experience living through one of the worst hurricanes in history. The letter told of their drive to Alabama to seek refuge when reports predicted a Category Five storm. They took shelter in the basement of a church and watched a battery-powered television all night. They drove back to Mississippi the next day. At the time they had no idea that Biloxi had been hit by unthinkable wind forces that had changed its landscape for years to come.

"As we made our way out of Mobile, we were shocked by the damage we saw in Alabama. The further we drove west, the more severe the damage became. Little did we know that nearly ninety thousand square miles were left a wasteland? We decided to go and check on the home of folks who had evacuated with us. We were only able to drive within a few blocks of it because of all the debris blocking the roads. We got out of the car and made our way up to their street, and quickly realized there was no home left. Only a concrete slab and two steps remained! We couldn't believe our eyes. We thought we might have been mistaken, but there was no mistake. Only the loud hissing of broken gas pipes brought us back to stark, brutal realty."

They drove to his medical offices next, and the building had experienced only some roof damage. Small amounts of water had actually entered into the clinic. All their patient records and equipment were fine. He breathed a sigh of relief and thanked the Lord. Then, they drove to their home a few miles away and found it unscathed. (Little did they know their home would soon become a place where the hands and feet of Jesus would minister to so many who had lost everything.)

They drove to their church and exhaled as they saw the fellowship hall still standing and how the tidal wave had stopped short of the church grounds. They were overwhelmed. Just a block away, miles of beautiful antebellum mansions along the coast had been completely swept away.

The disaster had touched everyone.

Disasters and the Devil

When I think of someone from Scripture who went through one disaster after another, I always think of Job. The beginning of the Book of Job tells us Job lived a godly life. He loved and respected God, and he hated evil. Job was the richest man around, and God had really blessed him. He also employed many servants and had ten children. (Personally I'd probably be questioning that as a blessing, but in Job's day a large family was considered evidence of God's rich blessing on a life.)

It's interesting that in Job 1:7 the story shifts to heaven. God required the angels to report to him periodically, and on this occasion Satan shows up. God asks him where he is coming from, and Satan says, "From roaming through the earth and going back and forth in it." (NIV)

The Lord brings up Job to Satan and asks him if he'd ever considered this amazing man. We can only speculate why God asked him that. Satan tells God he hasn't been able to touch Job because of the hedge of protection God has around Job.

This conversation illustrates many things about God and Satan's relationship. We know about Satan and his dominion from what the Bible tells us. In 2 Corinthians 4:4 Satan is referred to as the god of this world. In Ephesians 2:2 he's also called the prince and the power of the air. In 1 Peter 5:8 we read that he is a prowling lion, seeking whom he may devour. From these passages we know that Satan has a lot of power and authority, but he is accountable to

God. Thus, he isn't more powerful than God; Satan has to go through God before he can come after you and me!

This is very comforting. As his child, he has put a hedge of protection around us, and Satan can't touch us unless God allows it. Remember God allows Satan to only do things that will serve his purpose.

Satan challenges God's confidence in Job, saying that Job is only faithful because God has protected him. God responds by giving Satan permission to test Job—with one stipulation: Satan can't take Job's life.

Survival Mode

With permission in hand, Satan goes to work on Job. He causes one disaster after another. He takes away his cattle, kills some of his servants, and allows a fire to destroy all his sheep and even more servants. Job loses his camels and more servants, a storm takes down his house, and his children perish. Job is overwhelmed, shocked, and stricken with the deepest kind of grief.

I find it personally comforting that Job wasn't so spiritual that he immediately rejoiced over all his huge loses. He acknowledges that everything comes from God and its God's prerogative to take it away, but his recognition of God's right doesn't diminish his pain. As he goes through the grieving process, Job is shocked and hurting big time. He tears at his clothes, shaves his head, and falls to the ground, grieving was over his losses and then blessing the name of the Lord.

Then, the enemy comes again and attacks Job's health. The poor man gets boils from his head to the soles of his feet. Mrs. Job comes along, and she's really angry. She tells Job to curse God and die. (Personally I find it interesting that Job lost everything but his precious wife.)

Knee-Deep in Grief

As I think about Job's pain, I wonder if you have ever been knee-deep in devastating grief and someone comes along and throws you a one-liner? It probably wasn't, "Curse God and die," but it was a kind of platitude:

"Honey, time heals all wounds."

"The ol' devil's at it again."

"Don't forget God's in control."

"You need to let go and let God."

I don't know about you, but this kind of super-spiritual-know-it-all gives me a pain in an unknown location, especially when I'm in the pit of despair. That feeling helps remind me of when to keep quiet and when to lend a different perspective.

For example, author and speaker Dee Bestin lost her husband of many years to colon cancer. Her wise counsel has taught me a lot about ministering to people who are in what she calls high-tide grief. She detailed her journey through deep grief in her book, *The God of All Comfort:*

> "When you are in the middle of fresh grief and someone tosses you a silver-lining-cliché, it isn't comforting at all. In fact it is very hurtful and maddening. There is a time for that kind of encouragement, but not when someone is knee deep in sorrow. Instead, just hold them and cry with them and say very little."

Job was fortunate to have three friends who at first followed that advice. They were at his side for seven days and seven nights without saying a word. They mourned and probably cried with him. They sat in silence because they knew he was hurting beyond words. The trouble was these same guys went on to spend forty chapters giving Job false assumptions about God.

Lessons from the Ash Heap

Job had some lessons to learn in the ashes. He asks God why all these tragedies happened to him. But God never answered his question. Instead Job changed:

- He went from being in pain and having a victim mentality to feeling blessed.
- He repented for not believing that God cared.
- His brokenness was a result of his restless pursuit of God.
- He gained a more intimate relationship with God through all his pain and sorrow.

Lessons to Learn

What can we learn from the tragedy in Job's life and in the lives of other people who have been devastated by catastrophes? For one thing, God allowed the disaster. I don't claim to understand his ways because they aren't my ways. But in the midst of tragedy we need to listen to wise counsel, advice that lines up with God's word. It is normal to ask, "Why is he allowing this to happen to me?" Job asked God sixteen times, "Why?" But be assured our suffering has not escaped his eyes. He is intimately acquainted with everything that is happening in your world.

Job was a righteous man, yet he still suffered tragedy. Both are compatible with biblical Christianity. His suffering was not in vain; it had purpose and meaning. God blessed the second half of Job's life more than the first. He died an old man who lived a long, good life (Job 42:12, 17).

In looking at Job's story, I find it comforting that God is bigger than any test or temptation we might face. God is faithful and will not allow us to be tested beyond what we are able bear. Sometimes he will provide a way of escape so that we can endure it (1 Cor. 10:13).

The Surge and the Savior

Like Job, Doug and Lois learned that God is bigger than the storms of life. They were amazed at how many people quickly came along side to help. Neighbors, people from their church, people from all the surrounding communities. They showed up to help in any way they could.

"Our home became a refuge to over one thousand people during the next year. What an opportunity to share the Gospel of hope with folks who had lost theirs. Lois was in charge of all the meals, and friends showed up every day with bags of groceries to help feed them. When the FEMA trailers were delivered, Lois helped the crews clean them thoroughly so each family felt valued. She welcomed them with baskets of food. Their denomination sent funds to help these people with gasoline, fresh water, and non perishable items.

"It was such a privilege to be a part of what God was doing. In time, thousands of people descended into our area from all over the country to help too. They rolled up their sleeves and told us to put them to work wherever they were needed. So we did! Imagine? Many left jobs in order to come and help rebuild. They cut down trees, removed debris, put tarps on roofs, gutted flooded homes, repaired roofs, and hung sheetrock. They've hauled supplies into the community and have lived out the life hidden in Christ. It has been an absolute delight to watch these people serve Jesus and hurting people.

"We were able to open my medical practice on a limited basis on the ninth day after the storm. It was over a month before we could drink the water. I know God spared my office so we could minister to many folks unable to pay for medical help and medicine.

"The days turned into weeks and then months, but God continued to energize us so we could continue to help those in need. The entire experience changed our lives forever. It became a joy and a privilege.

Never the Same

Looking at both 9/11 and Hurricane Katrina, the surge of trouble often focuses us outwardly on what is most important, but more importantly it furthers God's cause to build His Kingdom by serving others.

What is your way of escape from the ashes of your Ground Zero or the devastation of a natural disaster? The best escape is running to God and his word. Adversity enhances the teaching of God's word and makes it more profitable to us. In some instances it clarifies our understanding or causes us to see truths we had passed over before. Martin Luther said, "Were it not for tribulation I should not understand the Scripture."

Wrestling with why can help us come to an understanding of where we stand spiritually. For example, the crowds asked Jesus about another disaster that happened when a tower fell in Siloam. They wanted to know if the people in that disaster were worse sinners than others. You know what Jesus said? "I tell you, no. Unless you repent, you will likewise perish" (Luke 13:3 NASB).

The Source of All Comfort

When we feel alone in the midst of calamity, our foundation is this: God never changes. He is in control and disaster brings us face to face with an unchanging God.

> When times are good, be happy; but when times are bad, consider: God has made the one as well as the other. Therefore, a man cannot discover anything about his future. (Eccles. 7:14 NIV)

Maybe you are going through a disaster today. You feel like you are walking through the fire, drowning in hopelessness and fear, or settling into despair at night like London fog. You are desperate like Job. Remember God comes to desperate people. The deepest comfort doesn't come from answers; it comes from knowing God and submitting to the changes he's allowed in your life. Someday your suffering will be used by God to minister to others going through the exact same thing.

And it all starts with one single whisper, "Lord, I have come to the end of myself. Please change me."

Our nation experienced extreme change through two disasters, yet God used it for His glory. But what do you do when disaster strikes because of betrayal from a husband? A husband who happens to be a pastor?

Notes:

1. John MacArthur Tape GC1341 on reliability of Scripture Genesis 32 "Jacob wrestled with what appeared to be a man, but was actually God (vv. 28-30). It may have

been a Christophany, a pre-incarnate appearance of Christ."

2. Nancy Guthrie, *Hoping for Something Better*, (Carol Stream, Ill. Saltriver, 2007) 26

3. Dee Brestin, *The God of All Comfort,* (Grand Rapids, MI Zondervan 2009) 86

4. Martin Luther from Quotablequotes.com

FIVE

Changed Through Betrayal

"It is not an enemy who taunts me—I could bear that. It is not my foes who so arrogantly insult me—I could have hidden from them. Instead, it is you—my equal, my companion and close friend. What good fellowship we enjoyed as we walked together to the house of God."
Psalm 55:12-14

I love to receive Christmas letters. I know a lot of folks think they're just an excuse to brag, but I enjoy catching up with friends who live thousands of miles from us. It's hard to beat me to the mailbox at Christmastime. One year I remember pulling out the mail and noticing the return address on an envelope from my friend Brenda. I hadn't received her Christmas letter in two years.

Brenda and I had met at a Bible study. She and I were brand new believers and hungry ones at that. We couldn't get enough of the heavenly bread. Each week we sat together and shared what we were learning. In time she told me that her husband wasn't a Christian. She had been so burdened for him, but praying faithfully. Brenda grew in her faith faster than anyone I'd ever met, and I loved seeing the changes God was making in her life.

As the years passed, they moved an hour away and our conversations became less and less. Occasionally we'd meet for lunch or call each other. During one conversation she told me she was excited because she and her husband were going to a large, thriving church. The pastor was a gifted, articulate Bible teacher. Brenda called several months later to tell me that her husband had received Christ. She was on cloud nine.

A few years later Brenda called to tell me that Greg was teaching a weekly Bible study and the class had exploded to several hundred people. In time, he was asked to consider moving to Missouri to pastor a small church in the denomination. Who could have imagined this incredible news? The years of praying were worth it all.

Before long they were moving to Missouri. I got Brenda's Christmas letter that year, and they were both thriving in full-time ministry. Greg had leaned into the pastorate while Brenda was heading up women's ministries. It was like a dream.

With Brenda's Christmas letter in hand, I sat down with a cup of coffee to enjoy her latest news. My heart sank like a rock as I read her opening line: "It is with a great deal of pain that I write this Christmas letter, but the truth must be told. I have been concerned for months because of Greg's sudden change in demeanor and attitude. He seemed distracted. He wasn't studying like he used to, and his sermons lacked power. I thought he might be depressed or was even having a nervous breakdown over the constant pressure of leading the church. However, there was no breakdown. He was having an affair with one of my friends! So far he is unrepentant and convinced he's found the love of his life. The church has asked for his resignation, and I have asked him to move out. I put our house up for sale, and I'm moving to Texas to live near our daughter. Please pray for us. This has been devastating to our family and a large community of believers." She closed her letter with this Scripture: "Friends, when life gets really difficult, don't jump to the conclusion that God isn't on the job. Instead, be glad that you are in the very thick of what Christ experienced. This is a spiritual refining process, with glory just around the corner" (1 Pet. 4:12–13, MSG).

I let out a deep sigh as I thought of my precious, hurting friend. However, the verse encouraged me. Brenda was trusting God in the midst of betrayal. I called her, and we wept together. She said Greg blamed her for everything. He accused her of gaining too much weight and told her she was a turnoff. A wise counselor assured her that the bigger the guilt, the bigger the blame.

She went on to tell me that she had made a very crucial decision one evening when she was alone. "Lord, I am not sure I can do this journey. I'm afraid." She said the Lord had spoken to her in her spirit, "I will do it through you, but you must first give it to me." In that moment of relinquishment, the burden was immediately lifted. She was flooded with peace.

Like Paul, Brenda was pressed on every side but not crushed, perplexed but not in despair, persecuted but not abandoned, struck down but not destroyed (2 Cor. 4:8). How did she keep going? It was God's internal surpassing power that sustained her.

Their house sold, and she moved away. She said it was the very first time in her life she had thought of her own needs instead of everyone else's. When she arrived in Texas, she'd prayed for God to lead her to a place to live. She came in contact with a wonderful realtor. She shared her current circumstances with him, and he helped her find a duplex. She moved into one side of it and rented out the other to provide her with some income. He asked her if she'd consider coming to work for him as his book-keeper. She accepted. She was no longer counting on the externals. She was counting on Jesus.

The Problem with Change

It was hard for Brenda to navigate her changing landscape, and all change is hard. Even change for the better can take some getting used to. However, change that we feel is not so good can ignite a whole host of negative feelings and attitudes. Whenever I am speaking with someone going through change, I tell them that in order to grow, we *have* to change. As much as we might like to stay put, God loves us too much to let us stagnate. So things are going to change whether we like it or not, we don't get a choice about that. What we do get to choose is how we respond to change. We can choose to become angry, bitter, and defeated, but it's just a detour. Disappointment is a part of life, but that's no reason to wallow in it. Feel it, acknowledge it, pray about it, and keep moving. Change happens.

Change can be a good thing. Think what it would be like if things never changed. What if our children never grew into adults? What if we had to eat the exact same thing every single day? (The Israelites tried that last one when they were in the wilderness, and the results weren't pretty.)

What if no one ever died? Imagine living in this sin-sick world for infinity? What if the Lord never changed us?

So, as difficult as change is, we have choices in the midst of it. We can run to the Lord and place our confidence in him, who never changes, or we can seek explanations. God is not one to force himself on us. He is waiting—for us to come to him like Brenda did. As James writes, "Draw near to God, and he'll draw near to you" (James 4:8 NASB).

What changes are you choosing to run away from? As Dr. Phil would say, "So how's that working for ya?" No matter how fast you run that change will always be there, waiting for you to come to terms with it.

Betrayal and Sin

When I think of someone from Scripture who went through dramatic change because of betrayal, I think of David. David was an amazing guy even as a youngster. The prophet Samuel said he was a man after God's own heart. He was a simple shepherd boy who killed the great giant Goliath with a slingshot. Then he was summoned to make music for King Saul to ease his troubled mind. But Saul betrayed David because of jealously and hatred. Saul hunted him down to kill him, but Saul failed. David went on to become a mighty soldier, and God removed Saul as king.

God anointed David, and David became the greatest king of Israel and a cunning diplomat. He also became an adulterer. You see, godly folks are just as prone to distraction, deception, and boredom as everyone else. Often they become arrogant because of their accolades.

One night, David sat on his rooftop, watching as a beautiful woman bathed. Some say that if David had been out doing his job on the battlefield, he wouldn't have been at home and able to watch a naked woman, who was not his wife, take a bath. But sin is alluring. Kay Arthur put it this way, "It isn't as though David's wife had a headache. David had many gorgeous wives waiting for a call from him to join him in the bedroom. But David wanted what he couldn't have." So he inquired of the woman and learned her name was Bathsheba and that she was married. That didn't stop him. He had one of his messengers bring her to the palace, they slept together, and then she left. When a few months later he learned she was pregnant, David, like Brenda's husband, tried to cover his sin and shift the responsibility to someone else.

David called Bathsheba's husband; Uriah, a faithful warrior; to come and see him. After small talk he told Uriah to go home (assuming he would have marital relations with his wife). But because Uriah wanted to honor his soldiers sleeping on the battlefield, he slept on the king's doorstep.

David got desperate and had Uriah sent out to the front lines, and eventually he was killed in battle. Bathsheba mourned the death of her husband, and as a gesture of nobility, David asked her to come live with him, making her one of his wives. But it wasn't noble; it was a cover up. David ran from God for over a year while living in torment.

Reaping and Sowing

Just as David was tormented with guilt, so was Brenda's husband. He called her several months after she moved to Texas. He was overtaken by guilt over his sin, his betrayal of Brenda, and the pain he'd brought to his entire family and the church. He asked Brenda if they could get together and talk about it.

But something had dramatically changed in Brenda after Greg left. She was not the same woman he had left in the dust. Jesus had become her husband, the kind of husband one only dreams about. He is faithful, true, and compassionate. He was her rock, her provider, and a very present help in times of need. She knew she could live without Greg for the rest of her life, and besides that she still didn't trust him. Trust is built through actions, not words. "Show me, don't just tell me," she said.

Greg moved to Texas and got his own place. He pursued Brenda. He started going to a counselor. He admitted he'd been deceived. He confessed to being arrogant, above reproach, and even bored. He felt all his needs had not been met.

Boredom—The Great Distraction

Like Greg, have you ever felt bored with your life or like your needs weren't being met? For example, are you bored with being married or being single? Are you bored with your house or bored because you can't buy one? Are you bored with your church, the pastor, the music, or the uncomfortable chairs?

Satan loves it when we are bored. He whispers, *"If only ...,"* into our minds. *"Pssst ... if only I'd married someone else. If only I had a different job, a new car, and a better church."* Most boredom focuses us on the externals we think we need to have a fulfilling life. The enemy begins to weave his cunning deception and introduces us to the very thing we think we have to have. If we act on it, it can destroy us and then, we have to figure out a way to cover it all up, so we aren't discovered and blamed.

The Cover Up

David was far down that path of destruction but thought he'd covered his tracks. David overlooked one detail. No one hides from God; he sees everything, and he knows our motives. The Lord sent Nathan to visit David. During Nathan's visit with the king, he shared a story with David about a rich man, who owns many flocks and herds, and a poor man, who only has a little ewe lamb for which he loves and cares. Nathan told David that a traveler had come to the rich man for something to eat and the rich man refused to take from his own herd but instead took the ewe from the poor man and used it for the meal. Nathan asked the king to judge the rich man from the story. David became furious. He decreed, "He has to make restitution for the lamb fourfold because he showed no compassion" (2 Sam. 12:6 NASB).

Then, Nathan dropped the bomb on the king, telling him that he was the rich man in the story! He pronounced God's judgment on David, knowing full well David could have Nathan killed for Nathan's very words. But David's heart for God convicted him of his sin and brought him to repentance.

"I have sinned against the Lord."

And Nathan said, "The Lord has also taken away your sin; you shall not die" (2 Sam. 12:13 NASB).

David didn't say, "Hey, it's not my fault. I can't help it. Sexual immorality is in my DNA." David's repentance, as recorded in Psalm 51, revealed a contrite, humble heart:

> Have mercy on me, O God according to your unfailing love; according to your great compassion blot out my transgressions. Wash away all my iniquity and cleanse me from my sin. I know my transgressions and my sin is always before me. Against you, you only, have I sinned and done what is evil in your sight, so that you are proved right when you speak and justified when you judge. Create on me

a pure heart, O God and renew a steadfast spirit within me. Do not cast me from your presence or take your Holy Spirit from me. Restore me to the joy of your salvation and grant me a willing spirit, to sustain me. (Ps. 51: 1-12 NIV)

Even though David repented, there were consequences. Nathan told him that God would curse his troubled reign. Furthermore, even though David's life was spared, the baby conceived with Bathsheba would die as punishment. David also suffered many other personal losses because of his sin.

Repentance and Reconciliation

Brenda suffered her share of losses because of her husband's sin, but she didn't put her life on hold. She continued to flourish as she trusted God for everything. Greg continued to pursue her. He asked her to consider going to counseling with him, and she agreed. He was quick to own up to his sin. He confessed it, repented, and asked for her and everyone in the family for forgiveness.

Repentance is an important part of the restoration process. "Repentance is not just a change of mind; it is a change of heart. It is an inward response, not an external activity. But its fruit will be evident in the true believer's behavior. Then you begin to live miraculously. You manifest the quality of life that baffles those around you." John Macarthur.

The healing process slowly began, but then, the unthinkable happened. Their only son, Steven, who had stayed behind in Missouri with his wife and baby, suddenly died in his sleep at the age of 24. An autopsy revealed a congenital heart problem. Devastation and grief overtook them. They took comfort that Steven knew Christ and was in heaven and that someday there would be a family reunion. But the loss was overwhelming.

Today seems far away from the day when Greg's sin nearly destroyed Brenda and him and everything around them. He and Brenda are still married. They are serving the Lord is ways that they had never planned. They counsel couples on the brink of divorce and share about the healing that God can do. Greg meets many pastors who have ruined their ministries because of sexual immorality. He leads them to the God of mercy, forgiveness, and restoration. Greg and Brenda also spend a lot of time visiting their granddaughter in Missouri, and Greg's relationship with his daughter, son-in-law, and grandchildren has been healed as well.

When we try to live the Christian life on cruise control, it often leads to failure, including moral failure. Another way to look at it is through the eyes of Major Ian Thomas, "The Christian life is not about our own capacity and ability, but about God's; not about who we are, but who he is; not about what we have to offer, but what he offers, which is all of himself, if only we are available to Christ as Christ was available to his Father."

Imagine Your Life as a Psalm

Betrayal is a deep wound, and it can be hard in the midst of the pain to find hope or even the faintest joy. If you have been betrayed, I would like to encourage you to get into the Psalms and let them minister to your hurting heart. David wrote over half of them. You hear his brokenness, catch his humility, and embrace his wisdom as he writes. How was he able to do that? Because David actually became closer to God after he sinned and repented than before he went down that road. That pain changed his life and his relationship with God.

Let David's words comfort you and heal you from betrayal. God has allowed this hardship in your life so that your beliefs will become more real and less theoretical to you. You can start living out of your faith in the real world. Imagine that? God is crafting within your life the words to a psalm, one that can become a precious healing balm to someone else going through the same kind of betrayal.

How wonderful it is when God restores a life. How fortunate God does not show us the future, especially when the future appears to be the end of something wonderful.

Notes:

1. Quote by Kay Arthur on DVD from Bible Study, *Anointed, Transformed and Redeemed* Bible Study (Nashville, TN. Life Way Press 2008)
2. True Repentance by John MacArthur, Tape 42, gty.org
3. Maj. Ian Thomas *The Indwelling Life of Christ* (Colorado Springs, CO. Multnomah 2006)123

SIX

Faith in the Midst of Change

---

*"Therefore I ask you not to lose heart
at my tribulations on your behalf,
for they are your glory."*
Ephesians 3:13

Picture yourself driving down the highway of life. You're living in Texas, and one day, you change lanes and end up in California! That's what happened to our family.

First, we were transferred from New Mexico to Texas. We'd just bought our very first home, a new one at that, in El Paso. Because the house virtually came with only a key, our empty dirt lot screamed for attention every weekend. We'd get up at the crack of dawn and start planting grass and trees before the desert heat melted our skin. About the time the lawns started coming up and the trees took root, we were transferred to California.

Like a lot of folks, we hadn't read a lot of good news about California in our local newspaper. We loved going there on vacation, but to live there never entered our minds or desires. My first thought was that we would end up living next to Charles Manson, and our children would have to go to a lockdown school. Then a *big* earthquake would hit and sweep us into the ocean and out to oblivion. Truth be told, I wasn't sure God lived in California!

We were so new in our faith that we had no idea that moving is one of the ways God redirects our lives for his purpose. We just responded to the call and headed to California. We bought a home in a quaint suburb in Orange County—for twice as much as we sold our home for in Texas. It was twice as small, too.

Within two years an acquaintance invited us to her church. It had a funny name, and the pastor had a funny accent. His name is Charles Swindoll. The church is the First Evangelical Free Church of Fullerton. Having come from main-line denominations, we'd never heard of an evangelical free church.

No one could have prepared us for what we experienced that first Sunday. We'd been warned to get to the evening service in plenty of time to get a seat. I was puzzled. *Get a seat?* I asked myself. *Really?* The churches we'd attended seemed to have too many seats—empty ones at that. We walked through the doors of the main sanctuary forty-five minutes before the service began and almost every seat—all nine hundred of them—was taken!

They had a big choir, and folks belted out the most wonderful songs that I had never heard before. People were clapping and singing at the top of their lungs. When Chuck got up to preach, everyone took out their Bible. Neither my husband nor I had one. The minute he began we were captivated. I had never heard someone teach directly from the Bible with a message that spoke directly to my heart. A couple of minutes later, a nice gentleman came over and handed us two new Bibles.

"These are a gift," he whispered.

After I recovered from shock, I held that Bible like it was a priceless treasure. I soon discovered it was priceless treasure. Chuck taught for forty-five minutes, and it seemed like five. We stayed at his church for more than twenty years.

Soon, I joined the choir and met one of the friendliest people ever, Tudy Witt. She asked me a million questions about myself and then invited me to her house for a luncheon the following Friday. (This invitation was really my first introduction to Christian hospitality, Christian friendship, and fun. It may sound ordinary to you, but if you've never grown up with it it's quite a life change. In fact throughout the years, I've heard remarks from folks who intimate that Christians are tight ol' fuddy-duddies, who are boring and often pious. I can assure you that none of my friends fits that mold. I've never known more genuine, heartfelt friendships until I became a Christian.)

At the luncheon Tudy and seven other gals were there to welcome me. I was so touched by this outpouring of hospitality. They were genuine and seemed so interested in finding out more about me. When Tudy called us to the table, we were told to find our place cards. I didn't know a thing about place cards to be honest, but it was all part of her plan. She put me right next to a gal whom she was sure I'd like, Marilyn Meberg.

Marilyn and I hit it off immediately. Before long we made spectacles of ourselves, laughing over our common likes and dislikes. I happen to love sarcasm, and I'm gifted that way. Marilyn has the same gift, but her wit is so quick that it's hard to compete. Later that evening Marilyn called our home to invite us to come for dinner the next weekend.

When we arrived, we were immediately aware that Marilyn's husband, Ken, and my husband could have passed for brothers. They looked so much alike. After the usual chitchat, we sat down for a lovely meal and found out a lot about each other's lives. I often thought, *How could four people have so much fun and love Jesus, too?* We learned that Ken and Marilyn had a daughter, Joani, who had died shortly after birth. Our daughter's name is Joani. In time our kids met, and they became fast friends, too. In fact Beth, their adopted daughter, was my daughter's roommate after college, and they were in each other's weddings.

Throughout the years we spent many summers congregating in their backyard swimming pool. Ken was in charge. He planned everything. He invited new couples to join in, and we all became fast friends. After a day lounging in the pool and snacking, we'd play some volleyball, have a potluck dinner, and sit by the fire pit as the sun set. Ken would lead a sing-along of favorite hymns, harmonizing and basking in the goodness of God.

We also ended up spending a lot of holidays together because our parents lived outside of California. New Year's Eve became talent night. Of course no one had talent, but we'd make fools of ourselves and laugh the night away.

Through the years our friendships grew deep. We came along side each other during the tough times and celebrated the good ones. These friends became our chosen family. Looking back, their friendship changed our lives and the lives of our children. You know I am so glad God doesn't show us what's up ahead, especially when he throws a detour our way. If we knew, who knows if we would stay the course?

Detours

Have you ever wondered why there are detours in life? If they take us somewhere we want to go, it's a great trip. But if they take us places we never expected, we never seem sure about this road we are traveling. God knows the way, he has everything all planned out, and he plans to take care of us and give us the future we hope for (Jer. 29:11).

There are a lot of stories in the Bible of folks hitting a detour. Take, for instance, Abraham. He didn't want to take his son, Isaac, up to the top of a mountain and sacrifice him, but God had a plan. And there is also Jacob, who didn't want to wait six years before God gave him permission to hit the road and head out of town from his manipulative, deceptive father-in-law. But God had a plan. How about Joseph? Did he feel like going down a well that led to captivity, prison, and then a palace? No, but God had a plan. He led him down a road to save the nation of Israel from famine.

As hard as it is to imagine, God allows detours to take us to places to accomplish his will. But before God does this, he usually changes us first.

Moses is another good example. Moses was born during a time when the children of Israel were increasing in population at a rapid rate. Pharaoh was afraid that they might help Egypt's enemies so he began a brutal time of persecution against them. He declared that all Jewish boys were to be killed. Moses's mom was desperate to save his life, so she put her infant son in a basket and floated him down the Nile River. When Pharaoh's daughter heard Moses crying for his mother, she rescues him. That's quite a detour. He's was in a whole different kind of environment and grew up in the royal household as an Egyptian prince! He was highly educated, skilled, and confident. He was an advocate for justice and had hopes of liberating his own people, the Israelites. But then another detour came because he messed up. He saw himself in a place of human power, ended up killing an Egyptian slave man, and ran away because he was afraid of getting killed for his actions. He spent the next forty years in the desert, tending sheep—a far cry from the royal life he had once enjoyed.

In time, the King of Egypt died, but the children of Israel were in still in severe bondage and slavery. They cried out to God for help, and he heard their cry.

In the meantime, Moses was tending his sheep and took them up to the mountain to graze. Suddenly an ordinary desert bush burst into flames but was not consumed. God had gotten his attention and spoke to Moses about the bondage of his people. He tells Moses that he's sending him to bring the folks out of bondage. You would have thought that Moses would be happy.

Now, if Moses had still been the cocky, ready-to-fight, power-hungry guy, he would have probably said, "Hey God, you have made one wise decision in asking for my help. I'm your man! Leave everything to me; I'll get 'er done. This is no problem for me."

However, when we have all the resources, the power package, and can do it, then God can't use us. He has to humble us first. You see, Moses was humbled in the wilderness. He wasn't the guy he used to be. His self-effacing response went something like this, "God, there is no way I can do this. I'm not capable. I'm not ready. I can't get my words out right. I make a mess of things." But God wasn't interested in Moses's ability; he was interested in his availability. He told Moses, "I'll be with you. And this will be the sign to you that it is I who have sent you. When you have brought the people out of Egypt, you will worship me on this mountain." (Exodus 3:12 NIV)

Then God used Moses to display His supernatural power to Pharaoh and set the nation of Israel free from bondage. Moses, the Israelites, and thousands of Egyptians watched as God's glory parted the Red Sea, so they could head to the Promised land.

Like Moses, God uses detours so test the quality of our endurance and take us to a new direction.

Enduring a Detour

The detour God had planned hit the Mebergs out of the blue. Like most of us, Ken was always battling the bulge, but then he started suddenly losing weight without trying. We were at the beach one Saturday, and Marilyn whispered to me that Ken had lost more than twenty pounds. I was jealous, but she was concerned because it was sudden and unexplained. He tried to rationalize it.

By December, he'd lost more than fifty pounds. We went to a wedding together, and the next day, Ken went to the doctor. We prayed it was something easy to handle. The doctor ordered some tests, and a tumor was spotted. They scheduled a surgery to remove it. Our whole gang waited at a restaurant across the street from the hospital while Ken had surgery. We'd no sooner ordered coffee when a phone call interrupted us twenty minutes after he was wheeled into the operating room. It was pancreatic cancer. Nothing could be done to stop it.

From the human viewpoint our prayers seemed unanswered. We gathered around his hospital bed, crying and holding each other.

"Why?" we all asked.

Ken was headed down a road he'd never traveled. So was his family. Jesus was right by their sides and so were their friends.

Holding on to Jesus

After fourteen months of treatments, experimental drugs, and prayers from all over the country, Ken Meberg died. The laughter ended. The celebrations were over; our lives were never the same. Like anyone who suffers loss, we wanted to reverse the circumstances and bring him back. It seemed way too early.

I can't remember crying so much at a graveside service in my life. Chuck did the most amazing job reminding us how temporary life is and about the faithfulness of God. None of us has perfect faith, so we hung onto Jesus, who is the Resurrection and the Life. We knew Ken was home now in the arms of the one who saved him.

The reception was somber, and words were hard to come by. We tried to reminisce about happier times, but no one was laughing. After the last dish was washed, the food was put away, and the last guest walked out the door, our community of brokenhearted friends hugged Marilyn. We hugged the kids and promised we'd always be there, and we drove away. Randy Alcorn quotes Hebrews 13:5 as he discusses how we should respond to those detours in life:

> You probably know dozens of people in whose lives God has used tragedy to produce beauty. None of us seek tragedy or welcome it. But I encourage you to resolve now that should tragedy strike ... or if it has already ... you will let go of your limited

perspective and let God prove to you that his promises are true: "Never will I leave you; never will I forsake you."

New Highway

Fast-forward five years when an organization known as Women of Faith came on the scene. They asked Marilyn to join them. Unlike Moses who needed humbling, Marilyn was humbled that God would allow her to do something like this. Her gifted communication skills and unique personality were now going to be showcased in arena events. She'd hit a detour, but now she was on a new highway. Since then she has written several books, some of which include stories of how her plans fell through but God's purpose prevailed.

Marilyn relates to audience members who have lost a child. She speaks to the hearts of moms who have adopted. Her personal heartache and loss are the bridge-builder to other widows. She encourages them to explore new beginnings and celebrate life each day. Her humor makes her approachable, but it's her testimony of trusting God in the midst of suffering that makes her real.

Marilyn has moved from California to Texas, but I'm so glad we moved from Texas to California and met her and Ken. Who could have known all that God would do in our lives through their faithful friendship?

Someday, I know we'll all be reunited in heaven. We'll be sitting at the feet of Jesus, singing. Ken will be there, and I have a feeling he'll be in charge.

Marilyn never questioned God's Sovereignty. She knew He had a plan and was willing to go where He led her. In stark contrast, when my trivial plans are interrupted I find myself whining and complaining, as though I am a victim of my circumstances. You will understand when you read the next chapter.

Notes:
1. Randy Alcorn quote, Facebook, 2010

SEVEN

Change of Planes

*"Whether you eat or drink, or whatever you do,
do all to the glory of God."*
I Cor. 10:31

I have interviewed a lot of folks about the subject of changed plans and interruptions. I appreciate what Priscilla Shirer had to say: "When God interrupts your life and gives you a new direction, will you go? Right now you are either on your way into an interruption or on your way out of an interruption because that is the nature of God."

However I confess, I don't like it when I have to change my plans. Only when I am on the other side of my interrupted plans do I see His Sovereignty and my stubbornness.

For instance, last year I was scheduled to speak in Michigan for a one-day women's event. When flying from California to the Midwest, most airlines fly through Chicago. If you're going on to another destination, you usually have to change planes. Anytime I fly through Chicago, I stay for a few days first to visit our daughter.

I got online and found a round-trip ticket for two hundred dollars. Thank you American Airlines! I was ecstatic. I planned on spending nearly a week with our daughter first, so I booked my cheap ticket.

Three nights later I awoke (when my brain cells began speaking to one another) and realized I had been looking at the wrong calendar when I had booked my ticket. Arrgh, it turned out that I was speaking for a retreat on the same weekend that I had scheduled myself to fly to Chicago.

Change of Plans and Plane Seats

The next morning I called the airline, and they were more than sweet and gracious to change my departure date for me—oh yes, but with one catch—it would cost me three hundred dollars. Plus, the only seat available was a middle seat. I personally don't feel called to the middle seat, but it was all they had. So I coughed up the extra money and made a resolution to look at every calendar I own before I ever make reservations.

My new departure was a Monday. As I boarded the plane, I found my middle seat and got my things put away, but before I could settle into my seat, the gentlemen at the window seat greeted me and introduced himself.

"Hi, I'm Rick. Where are you headed?" he asked.

I told him, and he hit me with another round of questions:

"Why are you going to Chicago?"

"Why are you going on to Michigan?"

"Oh, you're speaking? What are you speaking on?"

"Actually, I am speaking for a Christian conference, and I am going to be sharing how I came to know Jesus Christ as my Savior."

"That's nice," he said ever so politely. "I'm Jewish."

I smiled and pulled out a book in hopes of reading it on the plane, but God had a different plan. For the next three hours, Rick told me about his passion. He was a medical researcher, and he was on a mission to tell the world that a certain vitamin could revolutionize the health of everyone. He pulled out reams of research papers, clinical studies, statistics, and proof of his study. It was all very interesting, but I was growing a bit weary of his constant domination of my time. However, Rick never stopped talking, and he convinced me that I should consider taking this vitamin as soon as possible. If he'd told me he was a part of some multilevel marketing organization, I would have lovingly punched his lights out. But he assured me that I could buy this vitamin anywhere for two cents a pill.

Divine Dissention

As we descended into the Chicago area, I asked him a question.

"Rick, you are obviously a man who is passionate about your research. I can see you have spent endless hours on your study and have come to a conclusion based on all your information. But I would like to ask if you've ever made an intellectual decision to either reject or accept Jesus Christ as Messiah?"

He said he hadn't, but he assured me that every Christian he'd ever met was wonderful to him and the nicest people to work with, etc.

"I have just one question though. Why do most of the people in the world hate the Jews?" Rick, trapped in his window seat, was a captive audience. I was off and running. "Rick, you know the story of Abraham, Isaac, and Ishmael, don't you?"

"Yes ... Eh, but tell me again."

I began sharing with him how God revealed himself to Abraham and told him that he'd make him the father of a great nation. He said he would bless those who bless this nation and curse those who cursed it. Many years passed, but no baby came. Abraham was frustrated. God appeared again and told him his descendents would be as numerous as the stars in the sky and the sands of the sea. More time passed, no child was born to Abraham and Sarah. So she took matters into her hands and told Abe that he would have to father a child through her Egyptian handmaiden, Hagar, because she was obviously too old to get pregnant. So Abe listened, and eventually, Hagar gave birth to a boy. She named him Ishmael. Soon, an angel appeared to Hagar and told her that her son would be a wild one, free and untamed as a wild donkey. He would be against everyone, and everyone would be against him. He would be at odds with his brothers for the rest of his life.

In spite of Abraham and Sarah's unbelief, God made good on his word, and Sarah gave birth to a son, Isaac. Abraham, Isaac, and his son Jacob became the patriarchs of the Jewish people. Ishmael is the patriarch of what we know today as the Arab nations—and they've been at war ever since (Gen. 12–17).

Throughout the centuries after Abraham died, God blessed the Jewish people. He made them mighty and powerful. He blessed them, and he prospered them. He gave them freedom, the Promised land, and he revealed himself to them. He gave them the Ten Commandments and the law and showed them how to be forgiven for their sins. He also taught them how to worship him. But time and time again, they turned to idolatry and sinned greatly. Then, they'd cry out to God for help, and he would forgive them. But they continued sinning. Even though the glory of God filled the temple, they continued to sin. Finally God left the temple, never to return. He told the Jewish people that he would scatter them everywhere, and people would hate them and persecute them because of their disobedience (Deut. 28). (I'm under no illusion that I was able to remember all the history of Abraham and Isaac because I am so learned. I know beyond a shadow of a doubt that the words came out easily because God was speaking to Rick through me.)

"Rick, this is why Jewish people are persecuted down through the ages." I noticed he had a look of sadness on his face. "Rick, I love God's chosen people. They gave us the seed to the gospel. Rick, have you ever heard of C. S. Lewis?"

"Uh, I think my kids have read his chronicles or something like that."

"C. S. Lewis was a brilliant man, just like you Rick. He was a professor at Oxford in England. He'd been raised in a Christian home, but he did not believe in Jesus Christ. When he was in his late forties, he decided to investigate the claims of Christ and prove that Jesus was just another man. When faced with the overwhelming evidence, he had to make a decision: reject him or accept him. The evidence was too overwhelming, and he fell to his knees and accepted Jesus as Savior. His life was never the same. He went on to write about his experience in a classic book called *Mere Christianity*. This book is still widely read."

Rick pulled out his pocket Day-Timer and a pen and wrote down the name of the book and the author. "I'd like to read that book. Thanks."

Then, I asked Rick if he'd ever heard of Corrie ten Boom.

"No, I haven't."

"Corrie actually went to my church. She and her family hid thousands of Jews from the Nazi regime in a secret room in their house in Holland. They did it for quite some time. Eventually these Jews would escape the country and find freedom. One day, someone got wind of what the ten Boom family was doing and reported them to the authorities. The police invaded their home and arrested the whole family. They were transported to jails, and Corrie and her sister eventually were taken to a concentration camp. Her sister died a few months later. Corrie discovered her naked body piled in a back room of the infirmary. A few months later, Corrie was miraculously released. She later learned it was due to a clerical error. Years later, she wrote her story in a book called, *The Hiding Place*."

"Now that's a book I have to read," Rick said as he wrote down all the information.

My heart was pounding in my chest. "Rick, have you ever heard of Joel Rosenberg, the Jewish Christian who has written several bestselling books?"

"Why yes I have. My neighbor never stops talking to me about him. He keeps inviting me to come to hear him speak."

Instantly, I knew why my flight plans changed. It seemed that the hounds of heaven were after a man named Rick. When the Holy Spirit is after someone, they seldom get away. I'll never forget that encounter as long as I live. I realize now that the chance encounter with Rick had nothing to do with chance. I also confess I am still ashamed at how perturbed I was about him dominating the conversation when we first began the flight.

God's Plan or My Plan

My plans changed because of a simple mistake I had made. Have your plans changed because you goofed up? Have you been kicking yourself, convinced you are losing your mind? You aren't alone. But sometimes God interrupts our plans because he has a bigger plan. He certainly did for Rick and me on that plane flight.

Close Encounters of the Best Kind

I think most of us are fascinated by missionary tales of "chance" encounters, like mine with Rick. The Bible is full of them as well, and Luke wrote a wonderful story in the Book of Acts (8:25) about such an encounter.

In Acts 8:25, God took the initiative and directed Philip the Evangelist (not to be confused with Philip the Apostle) through his angel to travel south on the road from Jerusalem to Gaza. With little information but complete trust in the God who guides, Philip set out and encountered an Ethiopian eunuch and his entourage. Commentaries tell us that this man was probably a powerful man, possibly from the Sudan, and the chief treasurer of a wealthy kingdom because of its iron smelting, gold mining, and trade centers. He was returning to Meroe after a pilgrimage to Jerusalem for one of the feasts, and he was sitting in his chariot reading from the Book of Isaiah. The Holy Spirit told Philip to go up to the chariot. He asked the eunuch about his reading.

"Do you know what you are reading?" Philip asked. The eunuch responded by inquiring about the meaning of a passage he was reading from Isaiah.

"He was led like a sheep to the slaughter and as a lamb before the shearer is silent, so he did not open his mouth. In his humiliation he was deprived of justice. Who can speak of his descendants? For his life was taken from the earth."

Then the eunuch asked, "Please tell me, is this passage about the prophet or someone else?"

Philip then took advantage of the opportunity and told the eunuch the good news about Jesus Christ. When the carriage arrived at some water, the eunuch exclaimed,

"Behold water! What is keeping me from being baptized?"

Philip answered, "If you believe in your heart, then you may."

And he answered and said, "I believe Jesus Christ is the Son of God."

After Philip baptized him, the Spirit of the Lord snatched Philip away, and he found himself at Azotus (This town was situated inland from the Mediterranean, on the famous military route between Syria and Egypt, about eleven miles from Joppa and Gaza). He continued preaching the gospel in every city he came to.

For Philip it was one incredible encounter after another.

Acts doesn't say if Philip ever met the Ethiopian eunuch again, and unfortunately, I've never seen or talked to Rick again. He gave me his email address, but I lost it somehow. But God knows where Rick is. I did my part, and God is doing his part in Rick's life. But my encounter on the plane was God teaching me another life lesson: God divinely interrupts our plans, so that we can accomplish his will. It's like what Ian Thomas writes:

Every time you give yourself the right to have a problem or the right to worry about something, you give yourself the right to live your own life. However, if you adopt an attitude of total dependence on the Life of the Lord Jesus, the only life with which God will ever credit you, then no matter how threatening a situation may be, you can relate it to him. You can say, "Thank you, Lord! This is no longer my problem or my worry; it is yours."

May I encourage you not to waste the changes that come into your life? It's simply the way God works. They just may be an encounter with someone who is lost and needs to hear about Jesus. No one has ever seen God (John 1:18), but where he is, his glory is displayed. I hope Rick saw that the day we met on the airplane.

As I think back over my rearranged trip, it wasn't exactly hard missionary duty. I wasn't mistreated and I didn't experience any pain. But let me assure you, when my dreams for an intact family crumbled, it was the beginning of the most excruciating pain in my life.

Notes:
1. Priscella Shirer, quote from CD of Deeper Still Conference.
2. Major Ian Thomas, *The Indwelling Life of Christ* (Colorado Spring, Co. Multnomah Books 2006) 121

EIGHT

Changed for His Glory

---

*"Then call on me when you are in trouble,
and I will rescue you, and you will give me glory."*
Psalm 50:15

There was a time I had some misconceptions about the Christian life. One was the assumption that because we were Christians, our children would become Christians and we would become the hallmark of what a Christian family should look like. The second misconception was after we'd gone through a certain amount of pain we would be exempt from more. Since then I've learned a few things. First, it is impossible to become the hallmark for the ideal Christian family when there are sinners living under the same roof. Secondly, I am thankful God brings seasons of respite between trials and pain. On this side of heaven we will always have them. I have begged God to remove my problems, but instead they have been the very tool he's used to change me the most.

We were in one of those respites for several years and enjoyed every minute. It was the year I sent out a family picture with our Christmas card. It was taken in Hawaii when we vacationed together. We looked picture-perfect! As soon as I mailed those cards, our once happy family fell apart. With the exception of three brief incidents, we have never seen our son since. We have never seen our grandchildren. For obvious reasons I cannot go into the details. They don't really matter. What does matter is how God changed my life when the plans for our in-tact family fell through. It didn't happen overnight. It was a process that began with intense pain.

In the beginning I thought I was going to die. I questioned a lot of things. I questioned God, and I questioned how come we didn't see this coming. Some may call it denial. Satan, who is the accuser of God's children, attacked my husband and me brutally. *What kind of parents were you anyway? You must have done something really wrong! Some relationship you must have had if they left town without even saying goodbye.* The attacks were endless. And it was like the death of an entire family without a funeral.

The process that happened to us next is best described by author Nancy Guthrie :

> When our skin is pricked by a thorn, what comes out is what's inside: blood. When our lives are pricked by difficulty, what comes out is what's inside. For some of us, it is selfishness, pride, bitterness, and anger that come seeping out. For others, it is the fruit of the Spirit: love, joy, peace, patience, kindness, goodness, faithfulness, gentleness, and self-control."

In the beginning what came out was my anger. White-hot rage lurked right below the surface of my mind and spewed out of my mouth like a volcano eruption. Fortunately, it was when no one was around that I had these spells. I'd scream at the walls. It would also manifest itself in the form of nightmares. I would wake from them in a cold sweat with my heart pounding. I cried out to God to help me, and I rebuked the devil. Finally he'd flee.

I was too embarrassed and humiliated to run into folks at church. Surely they would look at me and think what a pathetic parent I'd been. I really had thought my faith would keep me from hurting so much and experiencing such things, but it hadn't. I was swallowed up in despair.

Uninvited grief had invaded my life like the swine flu. I couldn't eat. I lost weight. (Trust me, I usually have to pay someone to help me lose weight, but depression paralyzed my appetite.) I never shed one tear—until nine months after the breach in our once happy family. That day, I was as low as I'd been in decades. I sat alone in our family room, and my husband went off to work. I began reliving the heartache and missing those grandchildren, and I started to cry. My weeping turned to sobbing, and eventually, I was wailing so loud our dog jumped in my lap to comfort me. For the next several hours, as I wandered from one room to another, I cried nonstop. Eventually, exhaustion set in and I finally stopped. I've never cried since.

In the beginning of it all, God sent in reinforcements. Faithful family members and friends came through like the Red Cross. I don't know what we would have done without them. They held us tight, listened without commenting (no silver-lining clichés), prayed for us, and stood by us like a mighty fortress. They lavished us with care and took our minds off our sorrows by inviting us out to dinner, a weekend away, or an evening in their home playing games.

Our daughter and son-in-law were equally as amazing. Two weeks after our nightmare began they sent plane tickets to come to their home for Christmas. It was such a gift. The following May, our son-in-law arranged for my husband to meet him, his dad, and a friend in Pinehurst, North Carolina, for a weekend of golf. It was one of the best times of his life.

My godly father-in-law, who was a pastor and is now in heaven, showered us with love and insight. He said, "When I have gone through the deepest trials of my life, God has shown me my own sin. God has pruned me, so I can bear more fruit." At first, I didn't understand about seeing my own sin. But in time God showed me that adversity reveals the corruption of our sinful nature. I remembered the times when I was an arrogant young woman and didn't honor my parents. Instantly, I knew how they must have felt, and I asked God to forgive me for hurting them. God humbled me. Adversity caused me to grow in holiness, and it continues to do so. It is like what the writer of Hebrews penned, "He disciplines us for our good, that we may share in His holiness" (Heb. 12:10b. NASB)

When I was alone in my thoughts, I'd find myself falling back into discouragement—until one very special morning. Jesus met me in my sorrow. I was reading my Bible, and his words jumped from the page into my soul, assuring me, "He is close to the brokenhearted. He rescues those whose spirits are crushed" (Ps. 34:18 NLT). Psalm after psalm lifted me out of my pit. "You, O Lord, will not withhold your compassion from me; your lovingkindness and your truth will continually preserve me" (Ps. 40:11

NASB). Each day the grief lessened until one unexpected day when my grieving stopped.

I also discovered that Paul knew about God's faithfulness when he was hurting. "That's why we never give up. Though our bodies are dying, our spirits are being renewed every day" (2 Cor. 4:16 NLT). His words really encouraged me.

From that day forward, every time I picked up my Bible, I asked God to speak to me. I am still in awe at how he does this—day by day and year after year. It doesn't matter where I am in bible reading, even if it's the Book of Obadiah; God speaks to me and meets me right where I am. He ministers to me through the circumstances I'm facing. He wants that kind of intimacy with me. He took my mind off my broken dreams; fixed my eyes on him, who is well acquainted with suffering; and transformed my life. What began as a deep, dark tragedy has turned out to be the very thing that has changed me the most! I can honestly praise him today for allowing this long season of pain.

My family and friends were a bit baffled by the changes in my life. Some agree it was commendable, even beyond human comprehension. They'd ask, "How do you live without one of your children? How do you live without your grandchildren?" I'm quick to assure them of what I'm learning, but it has nothing to do with me. It's Christ in me who does the work. That's why he came. Without him we'd only exist.

He longs to do that work in you as well. It begins with relinquishment. Christ was raised from the dead that we might bear fruit for God (Rom. 7:4). He wants to resurrect our life from despair so we can bear fruit! Jesus told us, "If anyone is thirsty, let him come to me and drink. Whoever believes in me, as the Scripture has said, streams of living water will flow from within him." (John 7:37-38 NASB)

Nothing New About Parenting

I came across this little saying years ago about children, parents, and theories on how to raise them:

> I once had no children and six theories on raising children. Now I have six children and no theories on raising children.

It made me laugh.

I did my own study a few years ago about children and parenting. My study began with God, my heavenly Father. He is a perfect Father, but his first two children broke his heart. His first grandson was a murderer. To this day, his children continue to break his heart.

I read stories in the Old Testament of great and godly kings whose children were evildoers! I also read stories of evil, wicked kings whose children were godly. Go figure! I hunted for promises about parenting but only came up with wisdom and wonderful principles. But I confess, I was unable to find a guarantee that mankind can determine the outcome of another human being. The fact is God has given all of us the freedom to make choices. Some of us make sorrier choices than others, but the good news is God is our perfect Father. He alone is all we need. But we don't know it until he is all we have. He is the author of new beginnings and the finisher of our faith. So if you have grown up in a home with less-than-ideal parents, your heavenly Father will provide everything you need.

During this season of my life, I began to write down all the ways God had helped me get on with life. I have shared these at many conferences. I have met with moms throughout my travels, and they've shared their stories of unthinkable heartbreak. Yet many were quick to tell me that in this place, God changed them. What began as heartbreaking circumstances eventually ended with personal victory. I included these stories in a book I wrote to help other parents, *Ready? Set? Go! How Parents with Prodigals Can Get on with Their Lives*. It's a book of encouragement for hurting moms and dads. It's filled with hope and healing from Scripture, and helps parents move past the pain. It isn't a book about changing our situations; it's a book about what God does in the midst of heartache. I have been greatly encouraged by emails that I've received from parents halfway around the world who have read this book and said it brought them so much encouragement.

One thing I do know about the breach in our family. It isn't a hopeless situation. The last chapter hasn't been written. We serve a God who is able, and he is able to surprise us when we least expect it. I know there will be a family reunion someday, but it may be in heaven.

Presenting Myself to God

This perspective didn't just come naturally to me. In the past few years God has been teaching me a new way of living. Trust me, I haven't arrived—we never do. I want to grow closer to him every day. I heard a sermon a few years ago on Romans 12:1–2 that gave me a divine perspective on this thing called the Christian life and how to live it out: "Therefore, I urge you, brothers, in view of God's mercy, to offer your bodies as living sacrifices, holy and pleasing to God—this is your spiritual act of worship." (NIV)

We begin with the first word in the first verse, *therefore*. Paul is using the word *therefore* to emphasize how important the message in the previous eleven chapters of the book is. Without going back and reading them, it's easy to forget, so here's a little tour through those chapters.

In the first chapter of Romans, I learned from verse 20 that from the time the world was created, people have seen the earth, sky, and all that God made. His invisible qualities, eternal power, and divine nature have been made known to all humanity. So no one will have an excuse for not knowing God.

In chapter 2 we see that mankind is indeed wicked, and good works aren't going to cut it. The goodness of God leads to repentance. In Romans 2:16, it says God will judge the entire human race someday. He will judge fairly. I won't be able to blame others for my actions.

I also learned in chapter 3 no one is going to get an A+ for deeds done in righteousness on Judgment Day. How do we know? In verse 10 Paul writes, "There is none righteous, no not one," and in verse 23, "All have sinned and fallen short of the glory of God."

The pivotal chapter in Romans is chapter 4. Sin has to be paid for, and God had the payment plan, according to verses 23–24. "Jesus's violent death on the cross satisfied God's wrath over sin. The resurrection provided proof that God had accepted the sacrifice of His Son and would be able to be just and yet justify the ungodly." John MacArthur

In Romans 5:1, Paul explains, "Therefore, having been justified by faith, we have peace with God through our Lord Jesus Christ." I will never forget the day that I met Christ. I had peace for the first time in my life. Peace is a person. It is Jesus. He lives within his children. He is our peace. Do you know how to tell the difference between a Christian and a non-Christian? The answer is peace and no peace.

Paul continues in verses 3-4, "And not only that, but we also glory in tribulations, knowing that tribulation produces perseverance and perseverance, character and character hope." That verse has greatly encouraged me through my darkest hours. You see, our trials have a purpose. The section ends in verse 8 where Paul reminds us of the trial Christ went through for us, "God demonstrated his love for us that while we were yet sinners, Christ died for us."

Chapters 6 and 7 essentially tell us that the power of sin can be broken in our life. In Romans 6:14 Paul writes, "For sin shall not have master over you, for you are not under the law, you are under grace."

Chapter 8 contains some really awesome promises. In verse 1 Paul explains, "There is therefore no condemnation to those who are in Christ Jesus." And then in verse 28, "And we know that all things work together for good for those who are in Christ Jesus, and are called according to his purpose." Wow, isn't that wonderful? I love what the word *all* means in the original language. It means all—everything! How does that encourage you today?

The promises continue in verses 38-39, "For I am persuaded that neither death nor life, nor angels nor principalities nor powers nor things present nor things to come, nor height nor depth nor any other created thing shall be able to separate us from the love of God which is in Christ Jesus." Whew! Isn't this the best news there is?

I will summarize Romans 9, 10, and 11: Despite years of rebellion and rejection of Christ, God's covenant of grace is still extended to Israel today. In verses 33-36 Paul gets pretty excited and writes this doxology: "Oh, the depth of the riches both of the wisdom and knowledge of God! How unsearchable are his judgments and unfathomable his ways. For who has known the mind of the Lord or who became his counselor. Who has first given to him that it might be paid back to him? For from him and through him and to him be the glory forever." Amen.

And then we get to Romans 12: "Therefore I urge you, brethren, by the mercies of God, to present your bodies a living and holy sacrifice, acceptable to God, which is your spiritual service of worship." What Paul is intimating is in light of everything God has done for you, isn't it just reasonable to offer your body as a living sacrifice as an act of worship? When I look back at my life through that lens of Scripture, it makes what I'm going through pale in comparison to all that God has done for me and will continue to do. And to think, the best is yet to come: heaven!

Wherever you are today or whatever you are facing I would encourage you to take some time and consider looking at all God has done for you. In the midst of all you are dealing with—whether it's illness, betrayal, financial reversal, the death of a loved one, divorce, a rebellious child or whatever—just consider this: Offer your body as a living sacrifice to God as your reasonable service of worship. Allow the superiority of Christ to shine through your situation, so that others can see him. He will be glorified, and it will give great purpose to your life.

Now, while you are in God's waiting room you will not become discouraged and frustrated waiting for your circumstances to change if you wait in his word. There are many in Scripture who would tell you why this is so important:

- When you read God's word it will bring you joy (Jer. 15:16 NIV).

- When you memorize God's word, it will purify your heart (Ps. 119:11 NIV).
- When you meditate on God's word, it will bring you success (Jos. 1:8 NIV).
- When you quote God's word, it will defeat your enemies (Eph. 6:10-20 NASB).
- When you study God's word, it will keep you from shame (2 Tim. 2:15 NASB).
- God's Word is powerful and alive. It exposes our innermost thoughts and desires (Heb. 4:12 NASB).
- Jesus said, "When you abide in my word, it will give you confidence" (John 15:7 NASB).

In addition to getting into his word, I would like to encourage you to begin developing a powerful prayer life. It isn't a task to check off a list but a time to build intimacy with God. Jennifer Kennedy Dean puts it this way,

"Prayer is not an activity, but a relationship. Prayer is not a formula, but a life. Only when we have learned how to live prayer, breathe prayer, be prayer...only then will the power available through prayer be consistently manifested on the earth. God has ordained that prayer will be the conduit through which His intervening, earth-changing power flows from heaven to earth. Prayer is what sets God's will in motion on earth. You will be so encouraged by the way he answers your prayers and grows your faith.'

Before the Finish Line

As I look back over each story in this book and what I have learned, my hope is that they have brought you encouragement. There is purpose for everything you are going through. You may not understand it right now, but someday you will.

When we are honest with each other, we'd probably admit that as long as we can handle life, we don't give a lot of thought to needing the Lord. We love him, but we're doing fine. But when we hit a detour, a roadblock, or a dead end, we cry out to him to get us out of it. He often does get us out of it, but he wants to transform us more than anything else.

Many of the stories I have shared from Scripture illustrate this. Moses, Job, David, Martha, Mary, Paul, and Peter started out pretty self-confident and ready to take matters into their own hands! But the truth is when we don't have anything to offer him except filthy rags, then he's ready to deal with us. We can't make it without him. Do you need to say that? You can say something like, "Lord, I can't make it without you. I want a growing relationship with you."

Don't let heartache define your life. Allow God to define your life. The key is relinquishment. You have to let go of the plans you've had for life and give them to God. Let him work. It's the secret to the Christian life—"Christ in you, the hope of glory" (Col. 1:20).

What do you do when your plans fall through? You give them to God. Ask him to change you through the process. He'll bring you to the other side of this life change, and then he will redirect your life to display his glory to someone else going through the same thing:

Anyone who intends to come with me has to let me lead. You're not in the driver's seat ... I am. Don't run from suffering, embrace it. Follow me and I'll show you how. Self-help is no help at all. Self-sacrifice is the way, my way, to finding yourself, your true self. What good would it do to get everything you want and lose you, the real you. (Luke 9:23, MSG)

Notes:

1. Nancy Guthrie, *Holding Onto Hope* (Carol Stream, Ill. Tyndale House 2006) 17
2. John MacArthur, *The MacArthur Study Bible* (Nashville, TN Nelson Word Publishing Group 1997) 1770
3. Jennifer Kennedy Dean, *Live a Praying Life* (Birmingham, AL, New Hope Publishers 2003) 36
4. Dan Stone & David Gregory *The Rest of the Gospel* (One Press, Eugene, Oregon 2000)225

CONTACT INFORMATION
Judy Hampton
Email: Hampton917@aol.com
Website: judyhampton.wordpress.com